SILVERSMITHING
for
JEWELLERY MAKERS

Techniques, treatments & applications for inspirational design

Elizabeth Bone

SEARCH PRESS

A RotoVision Book

Published in 2012 by Search Press Ltd.
Wellwood, North Farm Road
Tunbridge Wells
Kent TN2 3DR
Reprinted 2012, 2013, 2014, 2015, 2016

ISBN: 978-1-84448-757-8

Commissioning Editor: Isheeta Mustafi

Art director: Emily Portnoi

Design: Emily Portnoi

Layout: Emma Atkinson

Photography: Xavier Young

Supplies: Cookson Precious Metals Ltd.

Printed in China by 1010 Printing International Ltd.

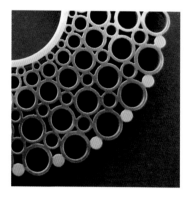

CONTENTS

SECTION ONE: TECHNIQUES AND PROFILES   4

SECTION TWO:
MATERIALS, TOOLS AND RESOURCES   174

SECTION ONE
TECHNIQUES AND PROFILES

Multi Form brooch by Adele Brereton. Photo: Victoria Ling.

Ring by Elizabeth Bone. Photo: Joel Degen.

Tall ring by Susan May. Photo: Susan May.

ANNEALING AND PICKLING

For silver to retain its malleability, it must be annealed when it becomes work hardened. Work hardening causes compression of the grain structure, making the silver harder and resistant to shaping. The annealing process of heating the silver and then quenching it relieves the stresses that have built up and so restores its workability. If work-hardened silver is not annealed and work is continued on it, faults and cracks will form.

ANNEALING

Annealing should be carried out under low lighting, because the annealing temperature is recognised by the colour changes of the metal, which are difficult to see under strong light. Use a torch with a bushy flame and adjust the size of the flame according to the size of the metal being annealed. The hottest part of the flame must be used; this can be found just beyond the tip of the blue cone.

A dull red colour indicates that the annealing temperature has been reached; this colour should be moved up the silver using the flame, taking care not to heat beyond this stage. The silver should be left to cool on a fire brick for a few seconds until it turns from red to black, or until the red fades. It should then be quenched in cold water.

Sterling, Britannia, fine and Argentium® silver each require slightly different treatments (see page 176 for more information about types of silver).

Sterling silver is 92.5% fine silver and 7.5% copper. It should be heated to a dull red, then quenched in cold water once it has turned black. After annealing sterling silver several times, there is noticeably less oxidation on the surface and the black colour stage gradually disappears. The silver should be quenched once the dull red colour has faded. Sterling is susceptible to fire stain caused by its copper content oxidising when heated. This penetrates the silver leaving a grey, purplish stain on the surface, which is more noticeable after finishing and can be hard to remove. To prevent this, avoid prolonged heating by using a large bushy flame to anneal the silver in the minimum amount of time and always pickle after each annealing. Coating the silver in a flux prior to heating will help to give it a protective layer. Depletion gilding can remove unwanted fire stain.

Britannia silver is 95% fine silver and 5% copper. Its low copper content makes it less vulnerable to fire stain. It is softer than sterling and can be worked for longer before annealing is required. It should be heated to a dull red, then quenched once the redness has disappeared.

Fine silver is 99.9% pure silver. It has no copper, so it won't oxidise, is not susceptible to fire stain, and does not require pickling after annealing. It is naturally soft and can be worked for a longer time before annealing is required. It should be heated to a dull red, then quenched once the redness has disappeared.

Depending on the grade, Argentium contains a minimum of 93.5–96% fine silver. It also contains copper and germanium and is fire-stain resistant. Argentium silver anneals at a slightly lower temperature than sterling and its colour at this temperature is a paler red, making it harder to see. It retains heat for longer than sterling and must be well supported and allowed to rest on the fire brick after heating – don't touch or move it until the pale red glow has completely disappeared or the silver may crack or fracture. Quenching too early can create the same problems. Some discolouration will appear when Argentium is annealed for the first time, but this can be removed by pickling. Subsequent heating should be free from discolouration due to the germanium present in the alloy.

PICKLING

Pickling refers to the cleaning of metal after heating and soldering in a dilute acid solution to remove oxides and flux from the surface. A diluted sulphuric acid solution of one part acid to nine parts water has been the standard pickling solution for a long time. However, acids are dangerous to store and use and it is now more common to use a type of dry salt called safety pickle. Safety pickle, like sulphuric acid, is toxic and corrosive; it should be mixed following manufacturers' instructions and health and safety guidelines. It is also important to follow proper disposal procedures for acids.

There are a number of chemical-free and environmentally friendly pickling options, such as alum. You can find alum under the name Fatakdi powder in the spice section of supermarkets: it is also stocked in chemist shops. Mix 30g (2tbsp) of alum with 0.5l (1pt) of water. Other chemical-free options include white vinegar with salt and a citric acid and water solution.

A warmed pickling solution works better than a cold one. Heated pickling pots or tanks are available in various sizes, but a cheaper option is to use a ceramic crock pot/slow cooker. The temperature should be kept on low and the lid placed on to prevent the solution from evaporating. Up to five minutes in the pickle should be sufficient to remove oxides and flux from the silver, but more time may be required if there is a lot of Borax or flux. The length of time also depends on the type of pickle used, the temperature, and the strength and age of the solution. The pickle will need to be topped up with water from time to time. Because the

pickle absorbs oxides, it eventually becomes saturated with them, causing the solution to turn blue. An increase in the time it takes to clean the silver is also an indication that the solution needs renewing. If steel gets into the pickle from tweezers or binding wire it will create a chemical reaction that plates the silver with a thin layer of copper. To avoid this, use brass, plastic or wooden tweezers and remove binding wire before immersing the silver. If steel accidentally gets into the pickle, heat and pickle the silver or scrub it with pumice powder to remove any copper from the surface. Once the steel has been removed, the solution can be used again without any further chemical reaction occurring.

After pickling, the silver should be rinsed thoroughly in water. You will need to agitate pieces that have hard-to-reach areas where the pickle might remain. Bicarbonate of soda neutralises the pickle, and a solution of 113g (4oz) of bicarbonate of soda and 0.5l (1pt) of water can be used to soak or boil pieces in. This is especially important where the pickling solution has entered a hollow shape. Dry thoroughly afterwards to make sure that moisture does not remain inside hard-to-reach areas. Additional drying can be done by placing the piece on some absorbent paper towel and leaving it near a warm heater or, for speed, you can also use a hairdryer.

ANNEALING AND PICKLING TUTORIAL
Annealing Sheet and Wire

YOU WILL NEED

- Silver sheet
- Charcoal block or fire brick
- Torch
- Water
- Pickle
- Silver wire
- Brass, plastic or wooden tweezers

THE PROCESS

1. To anneal sheet, place a sterling silver sheet on a charcoal block with the bench light switched off. Heat the silver using the hottest part of a bushy flame from a torch, moving it slowly and evenly over the surface of the silver.

2. Note the colour changes as the silver heats. A dull red colour indicates that the annealing temperature has been reached. Use the flame to take this red colour evenly across the surface of the silver, taking care not to heat it beyond this temperature.

3. Allow the silver to rest for a few seconds on the brick until the red colour fades and is replaced by black.

4. Quench it in water and place it in a warm pickling solution for up to five minutes. Remove the silver from the pickle when its surface is clean and matte white. Rinse it in water and then dry it.

5. Further heating of the same piece will produce noticeably less oxidation on the surface and the black colour stage will gradually disappear. The dull red colour of the annealing temperature will be harder to see.

6. To anneal wire, coil some silver wire with its ends tucked in to ensure it does not spring open when heated. Place it on a charcoal block. Switch off the bench light and heat the wire with a bushy flame from a torch. Move the flame evenly around the wire, drawing the dull red colour around the coil. Turn over the coiled wire and anneal it from the other side to ensure that any parts that may not have reached the dull red stage are heated properly.

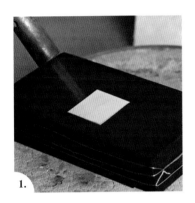

1.

2.

3.

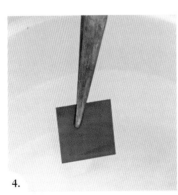

4.

5.

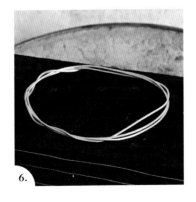

6.

HINTS & TIPS

Stop and anneal the silver once it becomes work-hardened; continuing to work on it can cause fractures and cracks.

Make sure that fire bricks and charcoal blocks are clean and free from pieces of solder because these could melt on to the silver during annealing.

Use a soft, bushy flame to heat the silver in a minimum amount of time. Adjust the size of the flame according to the piece or change to a different-sized torch head. Keep the flame moving evenly over the silver, ensuring that it is not heated beyond the annealing stage.

Always let the silver cool briefly before quenching it in water and pickling.

Larger pieces, such as cuffs or bangles, may benefit from being leaned against a fire brick or having bricks placed around them so that heat is not lost during annealing.

SOLDERING

Soldering creates a permanent join between two or more pieces of metal using an alloy of the metal called solder. The solder has a lower melting point than the metal and, with the use of flux and heat, it flows to make a join. Silver solder is made up of silver, copper and zinc in varying proportions and it is the amount of zinc that dictates the temperature at which the solder will flow.

The different grades of silver solder are hard, medium, easy and extra easy (there is also an extra hard grade for enamelling). Hard solder contains the least amount of zinc, so requires the highest temperature to flow; it is a good colour match with silver and flows well. (See page 187 for more information about soldering temperatures.)

As a general rule, always start with hard solder. Any subsequent joins on the same piece should be made with medium, and final joins with easy. This ensures that previous solder seams do not flow again causing the join to open up. However, each soldering job is different and should be individually assessed beforehand. Where there are multiple solder joins on one piece, you can use hard solder for a number of the joins, depending on their proximity to each other, progressing to medium and then easy for the final joins. Existing solder joins can be protected by making a paste of powdered rouge and water, which is carefully painted along the solder seam, preventing the solder from flowing again when the piece is reheated. Extra easy flows at the lowest temperature of all the silver solders and should be used for repair work. Silver solder can be purchased as sheet, strip or wire.

To enable the solder to flow, flux is painted on to the join; this absorbs oxygen keeping the silver clean and preventing it from oxidising. There are a number of suitable fluxes available, such as Borax.

A pair of steel tweezers, reverse-action tweezers and a soldering probe to pick up and move solder around are essential tools, as well as a charcoal block and fire bricks. A turntable allows the work to be rotated as it is heated. It's a good idea to have both a small and a large torch, or a torch with several burners to provide a choice of flame sizes.

SOLDERING METHODS

Chip or Pallion: This is the most commonly used soldering method. A fringe is cut lengthways up the sheet or strip of solder then small pieces – pallions – are cut widthways from the fringe. The pallions are applied to the fluxed join either before or during heating.

Sweat: This method is good for overlay and for hollow forms. It creates a neater join where the solder is less noticeable. Solder is run on to one surface, which is then soldered to another piece.

Probe or Pick: This method is useful where it is difficult to place solder prior to heating and also for repetitive jobs. The solder chips are cut, the work is fluxed and heated, then the solder is picked up using a soldering probe; dipping the end of the probe in flux helps the solder to stick to it. The solder can be applied to the work directly from the probe or can be melted into a ball prior to applying.

Stick Feeding: This is a good method to use on larger pieces or where a seam requires quite a lot of solder, such as in scoring and bending. A strip of solder is held in reverse-action insulated tweezers, both the join or seam and the end of the solder are fluxed and the metal is heated. Just before it reaches the correct temperature, the strip of solder is touched against the metal and the torch draws the solder along the seam from the opposing side.

Paste: This is useful for delicate work, hard-to-reach areas and some repetitive jobs. Solder and flux are ready-mixed as a paste and supplied in a syringe that allows a small dot of solder to be dispensed. This should only be used as a complement to other soldering methods.

BEST PRACTICES

- Joins should fit well and be tight fitting without any gaps. Hold the join up to the light to check it. Getting this part right means you can avoid having to go back a step later on if the join hasn't soldered properly.
- The metal and solder should be clean and grease free and the join area must be fluxed to keep it clean so the solder can flow.
- Pallions of solder should be cut in a variety of sizes on to a small piece of paper to keep them clean and to avoid losing them.
- Overhead lights should be dimmed or turned off so that colour changes in the metal can be observed more easily.
- Just the right amount of solder should be used – a small piece placed in the correct position will flow a long way. Additional solder can be added if needed.
- Solder should be placed so that it touches both parts of the join.
- Solder flows towards heat and in order for the solder to make a proper join, all parts, including the solder, must reach the correct flow temperature. The whole piece must be heated evenly, keeping the flame directly off the solder and join. Once the correct temperature has been reached, use the flame to direct the flow of solder along and through the join.
- Withdraw the flame as soon as the solder has flowed as overheating causes the zinc to burn out of the solder, creating pits in the silver and along the seam. The loss of zinc increases the melting and flow point, so additional solder should be introduced, rather than reheating what is left.
- Soldering hollow shapes requires extra care to ensure they do not explode. After soldering the shape, drill air holes at opposing positions so that trapped air or steam can be released when any subsequent heating is carried out.
- Don't use hard silver solder with Argentium silver because the melting points of both are very close. Use medium and easy silver solders instead. There are also solders that have been developed specifically for use with Argentium.

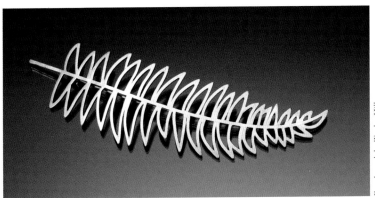

Fern brooch by Trudee Hill.
Photo: Douglas Yaple.

SOLDERING TUTORIAL
Chip/Pallion and Stick Feed

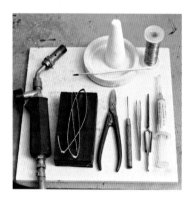

YOU WILL NEED

- Flat-band ring or bangle
- Sterling silver sheet, scored and folded
- Hard silver solder
- Tin snips
- Rolling mill or steel block and flat-faced hammer
- Small piece of paper
- Steel tweezers
- Reverse-action insulated tweezers
- Binding wire
- Wire cutters
- Soldering probe
- Files
- Scotch-Brite
- Emery paper
- Soldering brick and/or charcoal block
- Borax cone and dish
- Flux brush
- Torch
- Water
- Pickling solution
- Paper towel

THE PROCESS: CHIP/PALLION

1. Form a strip of sterling silver into a ring and prepare it for soldering. To check for gaps, hold the ring up to the light. Once a satisfactory join has been achieved, the join area can be cleaned with Scotch-Brite.

2. Cut a length of hard silver solder and pass it through a rolling mill several times to reduce its thickness. After cleaning with Scotch-Brite, use tin snips to make several cuts along the length of the strip, creating a fringe. Straighten out the curled fringe using flat-nose pliers. Cut small pieces of solder in varying sizes widthways from the fringe.

3. Mix the Borax cone with water to a creamy paste in the Borax dish to make the flux. Rehydrate it regularly with water to prevent it from drying out.

4. Place a piece of hard silver solder on the charcoal block. Paint flux on to the entire join area of the ring and place the ring with the join directly on top of the solder to hold it in position. (This is a good way for a beginner to start. Other ways include placing the solder directly on top of the join).

5. With the flame pointing at an angle down towards the ring, heat the whole piece evenly. The flux will bubble up, then, as the water evaporates, it will settle. When the silver becomes hot, bring the flame around to the front and move it from one side of the join to the other. As soon as you see a shiny line running, use the flame to direct the flow along the join, then remove it quickly.

6. Turn the ring immediately around and heat the inside of the join evenly to draw the solder through.

THE PROCESS: STICK FEED

7. Prepare a hammer-textured silver bangle for soldering by filing and making a good join, then securing it with binding wire to prevent it from moving and opening up when the flame is introduced. Use fire bricks to build a wall around the piece to prevent heat escaping. Paint the join with flux and place a pallion of hard silver solder along the inside seam to ensure that the texture on the front does not become flooded with solder. Heat the whole piece evenly, and once the flux has bubbled up and settled, nudge the pallion of solder back into position using a soldering probe. When the silver becomes hot, concentrate the flame on the inside and move it from one side of the join to the other. As soon as you see a shiny line running,

use the flame to direct the flow along the join, then remove it quickly. Before cooling and pickling, turn the piece and heat the opposing textured side of the join to draw the solder through from the inside.

8. Clean and cut a strip of hard silver solder and hold it in a pair of reverse-action tweezers. Clean a scored and folded seam and then flux both the seam and the end of the solder. Heat the silver and, when it almost reaches soldering temperature, touch the strip of solder against the edge of the metal at the seam and use the torch from the opposite side to draw the solder flow along the seam.

HINTS & TIPS

Anneal work-hardened silver before soldering as the join may open up as the silver softens with the heat.

To prevent solder flowing into textured surfaces, take extra precautions, such as soldering from the reverse side.

Build a wall with soldering bricks around larger pieces to prevent heat from escaping.

If a solder seam comes apart, clean and file it before resoldering it.

To find a soldered join, gently heat the piece with a soft flame. The solder seam will eventually show as a dark line or discoloured area.

Don't be tempted to use too big a piece of solder for a particular join. It is easier to add more solder later if necessary than it is to file away excess.

Try to keep soldering as brief as possible. Hard solder melts at a temperature close to that of annealing, so the silver may look red.

4.

5.

7.

8.

SOLDERING TUTORIAL
Hollow Shape, Butt Join and Cuff-link Fitting

YOU WILL NEED

- Silver sheet, silver wire, cuff-link fitting
- Hard and medium silver solder
- Tin snips
- Rolling mill or steel block and flat-faced hammer
- Small piece of paper
- Steel tweezers
- Reverse-action insulated tweezers
- Soldering probe
- Flat-hand, round-needle and barette-needle files
- Scotch-Brite
- Emery paper
- Powdered rouge
- Small paintbrush
- Soldering bricks and/or charcoal block
- Borax cone and dish
- Flux brush
- Torch
- Water
- Pickling solution
- Paper towel
- Small drill bit
- Pin vice or pendant motor

THE PROCESS: HOLLOW SHAPE

1. Form a narrow strip of silver sheet into a small ring and solder it using hard silver solder as in Steps 2–6 on page 12. File and true it on an oval mandrel. File and paper both edges straight.

2. Cut two pieces of silver sheet a little larger than the prepared oval ring; hammer the sheets flat and then paper them. Place one piece on a charcoal block and flux it. Place the oval ring on top, with its solder seam positioned at the back and away from the direction of the flame. Put small pallions of hard silver solder on the sheet and around the outside of the oval ring with their edges touching its wall. Don't place solder against the solder seam of the oval ring.

3. Heat the piece, concentrating the heat around the edge of the sheet and keeping the flame moving and avoiding playing it directly on the oval ring. As the flat sheet becomes hot, this in turn will heat the oval ring. The flux will bubble up and settle. Nudge any pallions of solder that move out of position with a soldering probe. Once the entire piece has become hot, play the flame around one side at an angle, concentrating it on the area of the join. As soon as one pallion of solder starts flowing, use the flame to lead the flow to the next pallion and so on, until a shiny silver line is seen flowing, completing the solder join.

4. After cooling, quenching, pickling and drying, cut the sheet and file it back to the wall of the oval ring. Mix powdered rouge to a paste with a little water and carefully paint it along the solder seam and allow it to dry. Complete the hollow shape by soldering the piece to the second piece of prepared sheet, as in Steps 2 and 3, using medium silver solder.

5. When the hollow shape is quenched, look for air bubbles rising – this indicates that the solder may not have flowed properly to seal the join. Drill two small holes in opposing positions to release air and any trapped liquid.

THE PROCESS: BUTT JOIN

6. Create a groove at one end of a piece of silver wire using a round-needle file. Place the prepared end along the length of another piece of wire with the same diameter, adjusting the groove to achieve a good fit.

7. Set up both wires on a flat charcoal block. Paint flux on to the join area and position a pallion of hard solder so that it touches both pieces. Heat both parts evenly, keeping the flame off the solder until the moment it flows.

8. After cooling, quenching, pickling and drying, refine the join using a barette-needle file, followed by emery paper.

THE PROCESS: CUFF-LINK FITTING

9. Hold a silver cuff-link fitting in reverse-action tweezers, apply flux and a pallion of hard solder to the prepared end, and heat it. Remove the flame quickly at the moment the solder melts. Flux the silver shape on the back and preheat it, then carefully position the fitting and heat both parts until the solder flows to form the join.

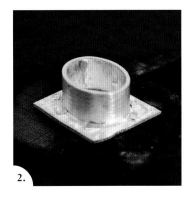

2.

3.

4.

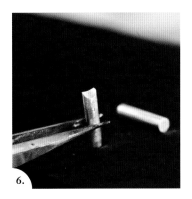

6.

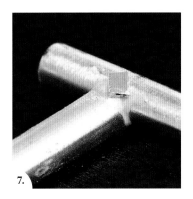

7.

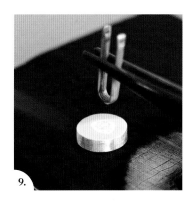

9.

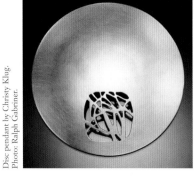

CUTTING AND FILING

Cutting and filing are essential techniques for silversmithing. Once mastered, these skills will be used again and again in almost every area of silver jewellery making.

CUTTING

Guillotines, shears and tin snips can all be used to cut sheet silver, but the cut produced by these tools will not be particularly accurate and will leave a distorted edge. Wire can be cut with top or side wire cutters, both of which leave a distorted end that needs filing. Flush cutters leave a clean end on the wire that requires little cleaning up.

Sheet, wire and tube can be cut using a jeweller's saw, which produces a more accurate cut. A saw is an essential and versatile tool that can be used for both basic and intricate cutting. The saw consists of a frame into which a fine blade is set. The blade works on tension, so there must be no flexibility in it while cutting. Blades are available in a variety of sizes from 4/0, the

thickest, to 8/0, the finest. The choice of blade depends upon the thickness of the metal to be cut; but as a general rule there should be three teeth to the thickness of metal. As a guide, 4/0–8/0 is suitable for fine work and piercing thinner sheet up to 22-gauge (0.6mm); 3/0 is suitable up to 16-gauge (1.3mm); 2/0 is suitable up to 14-gauge (1.6mm); 1–4 is suitable for thicker sheet up to about 9-gauge (3mm). A finer blade is easier to use when cutting curves.

The saw can also be used for decorative effects, such as creating fine lines and fretwork. Fretwork describes the cutting out of an area within a sheet of metal without cutting in from the edge and it is often used to produce intricate patterns. After transferring a design

to the metal, small holes are drilled close to the edges of the shapes to be cut out, the saw blade is secured at the bottom of the frame with the other end threaded through the hole, and then secured at the top. The saw is then used vertically to cut just inside the line, allowing enough room for cleaning up with files afterwards. The internal shapes should be cut first so that the metal remains comfortable to hold.

A bench peg is essential when using the jeweller's saw and it should have a V-shape cut out from it. Use your primary hand to hold the saw, while your secondary hand supports the metal against the bench peg, with smaller pieces being held and cut towards the top of the V.

FILING

Filing is used to shape, refine, remove defects and burrs, enlarge holes and create grooves. A file is made from steel and has teeth that cut into the metal as it files. They are available in various grades from very rough-cut 00 to smooth-cut 4. The various types of files are:

- Hand Files: These are the largest files and are available in various shapes in either 15cm (6in) or 20cm (8in) lengths. A flat-hand file in cut 2 and a half-round ring file in cut 2 are the most useful, as well as a flat-hand file in a rougher cut for quickly removing large amounts of metal. Wooden handles make the files more comfortable to use. These are sold separately and are fitted to the file by heating the tang of the file with a torch flame until it is red hot and then pushing the tang into the wooden handle and tapping the handle on a firm surface until it is in place.
- Needle Files: These are much narrower and smaller than hand files and are ideal for cleaning up small or intricate pieces, such as fretwork. They are available in different shapes and cuts; a set of 12 assorted shapes in cut 2 is a wise investment.

- Riffler Files: These are similar in size to needle files, with shaped and curled file ends that are suitable for intricate work, awkward shapes and hard-to-reach areas.
- Escapement Files: These are smaller and finer than needle files. They are ideal for fine work and stone setting.

It's important to use the correct file for the job. For example, use a round file for a hole, a half-round ring file for the inside of a ring and a flat-hand file for the outside of a flat-band ring. Use a rough file to remove a lot of metal and a smoother one to remove the marks made by the rough file. Always bear in mind that file marks will need to be removed with abrasive papers.

Never file a piece that is not supported, as this will result in poor filing. For long flat edges, secure the piece in a bench vice where possible, hold other pieces by hand using a bench peg to support the work as it is filed.

The file cuts on the forwards stroke using pressure from the index finger placed on top of the file. A long forwards stroke should be used with the file lifting up and away from the metal as it is brought back. If the file must remain in contact with the metal on the backwards stroke, then the pressure should be released. Be aware of the position of the file as it makes contact with the metal. Inspect the filed area closely, especially if a straight edge is being prepared for joining prior to soldering. If the filed area does not look smooth, then your filing technique needs to be improved. When filing curved areas, the file should follow the form to prevent the curve becoming flat. A jeweller's saw blade can be used to file with by using the blade with a stroking action against the edge of the metal to file and refine. This is particularly useful for refining sharp points inside fretwork shapes.

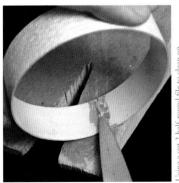

Using a cut 2 half-round file to clean up a soldered seam inside a bangle.

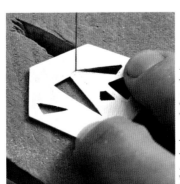

Refining the shapes of a fretwork piece using a piercing saw.

Cutting silver sheet with tin snips.

FILING TUTORIAL

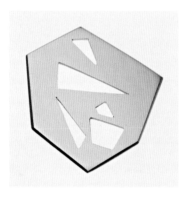

YOU WILL NEED

- Silver pieces that require filing: strip of sheet, flat-band ring, fretwork piece
- Flat-hand file, cut 2
- Half-round ring file, cut 2
- Barrette-needle file, cut 2
- Bench peg

THE PROCESS

1. File both ends of a strip of sterling silver sheet in preparation for joining and soldering together to create a flat-band ring. First, use a square and scribe to mark an accurate line to work to on the silver. Holding the strip against the bench peg for support, use a cut 2 flat-hand file to file the end straight and flat. Hold the file with your index finger resting on the top; as the file makes contact with the metal, increase the pressure from your finger. Use the whole length of the file and, as the file comes to the end, lift it up and away from the metal as the backwards stroke is made. Repeat this several times.

2. Inspect the end of the strip regularly to check that the file is creating a smooth finish across the silver. Turn the strip so that the end is filed from the other side to counteract any discrepancies made with the pressure and angle of the file. File the opposing end in the same way.

3. After soldering the ends together, remove any solder from the inside of the join using the curved side of a cut 2 ring file. Hold the ring against the bench peg and hold the file with your index finger on top. This time the backwards stroke is made while the file is still in contact with the metal. Turn the ring so that the file is used from both sides.

4. After truing the ring on a mandrel, file away excess solder from the seam on the outside of the ring using a cut 2 flat-hand file. Use the same filing technique as in Step 1, except this time the file follows the curved form of the ring so that flat areas are not created on it. File around the whole ring in this way; when the file has travelled around the ring once, turn it and file in the opposing direction.

5. Create a chamfered edge using a cut 2 flat-hand file. Supporting the piece against the bench peg, use the file to alter the angle along the edge with long forward strokes, making sure that the file does not make contact with the metal on the backwards stroke.

6. File up a fretwork shape using a cut 2 barrette-needle file. This can reach inside and up to the corners of the shape without damaging nearby edges. Keep the file in contact with the metal on the backwards stroke, but release any pressure exerted on the file.

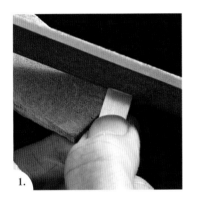

1.

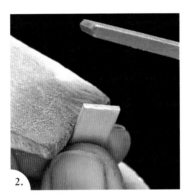

2.

3.

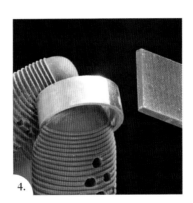

4.

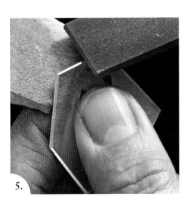

5.

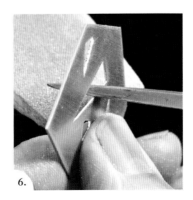

6.

HINTS & TIPS

Remember that files cut on the forwards stroke.

When filing flat edges, mark a straight line to work to with a square and scriber.

Always support the work. Long straight pieces can be supported in a bench vice. Hold smaller pieces by hand and use the bench peg to support the work or your hand.

When filing straight edges, make sure that the file does not dip at the beginning and end of the cutting stroke. This is very easily done and will create an uneven edge.

Choose the file to match the profile of the piece. Flat files should be used for convex shapes.

To file sharp points inside fretwork, use a jeweller's saw and stroke the blade along the metal to file and refine the point.

Store files separately; damage occurs to them if they are allowed to rub together.

DRILLING A HOLE TUTORIAL
Bench Drill, Pendant Drill, Pin Vice and Countersinking

YOU WILL NEED

- Twist drill bits
- Bench drill
- Pendant motor
- Pin vice
- Centre punch
- Block of wood
- Safety glasses
- Mallet or jobbing hammer
- Steel block
- Beeswax or burr-life lubricant
- Small drill press vice
- Ball or bud burr

THE PROCESS: BENCH DRILL

1. Secure the piece in a small drill press vice. To prevent the drill bit from wandering around on the surface, make a small indent by tapping a centre punch gently with a jobbing hammer at the exact location for the hole.

2. Secure a drill bit in the chuck of a bench drill and position the indent made by the centre punch directly underneath the tip of the drill bit. While firmly holding down the vice with one hand, lower the drill bit to make contact with the piece and apply a little pressure for the drill to start cutting into the silver. Drill the hole bit by bit, raising and lowering until the desired depth has been achieved.

THE PROCESS: PENDANT MOTOR

3. To enable a shape to be pierced from a sheet of silver, drill a hole for the saw blade to pass through. After marking out the design and position of the hole, place the piece on a steel block and use the centre punch to create a small indent as in Step 1.

4. Secure the drill bit in the chuck of a pendant motor. Working on a block of wood, hold the silver sheet down firmly with one hand while the pendant drill is held at 90° to the piece and firm pressure is applied for the drill to cut through the metal a little at a time.

THE PROCESS: PIN VICE

5. Prepare a piece of silver sheet for drilling as in Step 1. Secure the drill bit in a pin vice and, holding the rotating wooden knob in the palm of your hand, use your thumb and index finger to rotate the pin vice, keeping it upright and applying gentle pressure to drill the hole bit by bit.

THE PROCESS: COUNTERSINKING

6. To countersink a drilled or already existing hole, such as tube, use a ball or bud burr in a pendant motor to open out the top of the hole.

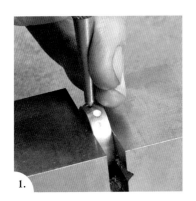

1.

2.

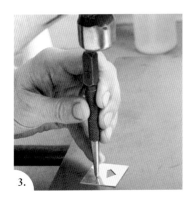

3.

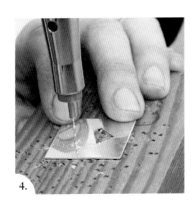

4.

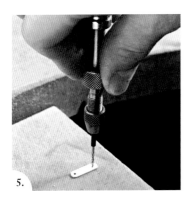

5.

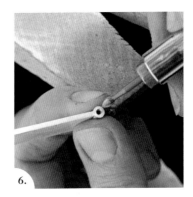

6.

HINTS & TIPS

Always wear safety glasses when drilling.

To protect the workbench, use a block of wood to drill on.

When using a pendant motor or pin vice to drill a hole, make sure that they are held at a 90° angle to the work.

Drill large holes in stages – start with a smaller drill and gradually increase the size of the drill.

Remove the metal swarf created when drilling by turning the drill in the opposite direction.

Drilled holes have sharp edges, which can be removed by enlarging the hole slightly using a ball or bud burr in the pendant motor.

Lubricate the drill bit with beeswax or burr-life lubricant to help it stay sharp for longer. This will also help prevent it from overheating, getting stuck and breaking.

PIERCING SAW TUTORIAL
Fretwork and Cutting a Straight Line

YOU WILL NEED

- Silver sheet
- Double-sided tape
- Scissors
- Jeweller's saw
- Saw blades
- Beeswax (to ease the blade)
- Bench peg with a V-shape cutout
- Small twist drill bit 1mm (½in) or less
- Pin vice, bench drill or pendant motor

THE PROCESS: FRETWORK

1. Print a design on paper and cover it in double-sided tape, then cut out and apply it to a piece of sterling silver sheet. Drill small holes close to the edges of the shapes to be cut out.

2. Sitting at the bench, hold the handle of the saw frame against your chest with the other end against the bench peg so that both hands are free. With its teeth uppermost and running down towards the handle, secure the blade in the bottom clamp. Then insert the blade through one of the holes in the silver sheet, with the design facing upwards.

3. Allow the silver to fall to the bottom of the blade and push the frame against the bench while the blade is secured in the top clamp. When the pressure is released, the blade becomes tense.

4. Check the blade was loaded correctly by carefully running an index finger down the teeth in the direction of the saw frame handle. Your finger should travel smoothly down without catching.

5. Using your primary hand, grip the saw frame handle lightly and keep the saw vertical while your secondary hand holds the silver sheet firmly on the bench peg and over the cutout V-shape. Hold the saw frame at a slight angle to start the cut, then return it to a vertical position. Continue cutting using long, even strokes up and down; keep the blade vertical and use little force.

6. Cut curves by slowly turning the piece towards the saw with your secondary hand. Cut pointed shapes by sawing up to the point from one side, then sawing backwards to the blade entry hole, then sawing in the opposite direction to the point. Once all the internal shapes have been pierced out, the outside shape can be cut. Use needle files to refine the edges.

THE PROCESS: CUTTING A STRAIGHT LINE

7. Secure a blade in the top of the frame, then push the frame against the bench peg while the blade is secured at the bottom. Check the blade tension and the direction of the teeth. Working on the bench peg at the top of the V, hold the frame at a slight angle to start the cut, then return it to a vertical position as the straight line is cut using long, even strokes up and down, keeping the blade vertical and using little force. Turn the corners by keeping the blade moving up and down in one place, not forcing it forwards, and at the same time turning both the saw and metal.

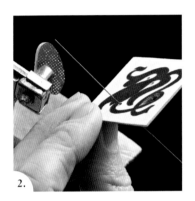

2.

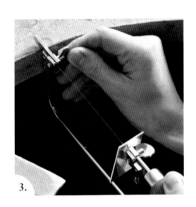

3.

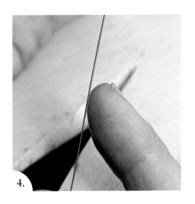

4.

5.

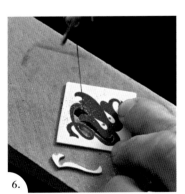

6.

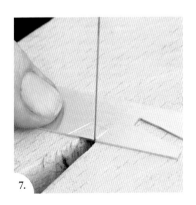

7.

HINTS & TIPS

The cutting motion comes from your elbow, not your wrist. Hold the saw frame lightly with a relaxed arm and body and use long, even strokes.

Blades can be easily broken if too much force is used or if the wrong blade is used for the thickness of metal.

Always check the tension of the blade: a loose blade will break.

Tilt the blade at a slight angle to start a cut, then return it to a vertical position to continue.

Always support the work with your secondary hand to prevent it from flapping with the cutting action. Keep your fingers out of the path of the saw.

The bench peg should have a V-shape cutout for use with the piercing saw. Smaller pieces should be held and cut in the safer area towards the top of the V.

Arm Sculpture by Ute Decker. Photo: Elke Bock.

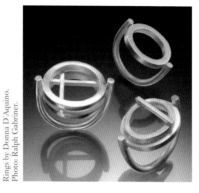

Rings by Donna D'Aquino. Photo: Ralph Gabriner.

Ring by Melanie Ihnen. Photo: Orlando Luminere.

BASIC FORMING

Basic forming uses techniques that quickly bend sheet and wire into simple or more complex forms for jewellery. Ring shanks and bangles are examples where basic forming is utilised.

TOOLS FOR FORMING

Pliers, mandrels and rawhide or nylon mallets are essential tools for this technique. It is also useful to have a good range of pliers with different profiles. Flat-nose, snipe-nose and parallel pliers are used for bending angles; half-round pliers are used for making curves and are useful when starting to bend a strip of sheet to form a ring shank; round-nose pliers are used for forming tighter curves and are particularly useful for wire.

Pliers can easily mark silver, so they should be used with care to minimise damage: extra care should be taken with fine silver, because it is soft,

and with textured surfaces. The risk of marking the silver can be reduced by wrapping masking tape or leather around the jaws of the pliers. Some pliers are available with nylon jaws.

A rawhide or nylon mallet will not damage the silver and can be used for the basic forming of ring shanks and bangles by hammering the metal around a steel mandrel. Mallets are usually flat-faced and are available in various sizes; in addition to flat-faced mallets, there are also pear-shaped mallets. A new mallet will need to have its varnished head softened by hammering it against concrete or a similar rough surface before using it for the first time.

Basic forming often involves using a combination of mallets, mandrels, stakes and pliers. A certain amount of bending can also be achieved using your fingers and then using other tools to complete or refine the form. Silver should be annealed both before forming and again once it becomes work hardened and before any subsequent forming.

MATERIALS FOR FORMING

Material costs can be reduced when forming rings and bangles in silver by taking time to work out the length of metal required. A bangle sizer, a strip of paper or a tape measure can be used to measure and work out the length of silver required to make a bangle. Ring sizers that are similar to the ring you want to make should be used for measuring the finger. For example, a wide flat-band ring will require a wide-band ring sizer. Wider rings will need to be made larger than a narrow band ring to allow for the width of the ring to fit over the knuckle. The thickness of the metal should be measured, doubled and added to the length of silver. (See page186 for a chart of standard ring sizes.) Binding wire can be used to help estimate the length of metal required for a ring. Wind the wire tightly around the ring mandrel at the correct finger size, slide it off and cut the circle of wire open and straighten it out. Use the length plus a little extra to measure the amount of silver required.

Alphabet rings by Trudee Hill. Photo: Douglas Yaple.

Starting to form a length of wire against a mandrel with a mallet.

Tapping a ring into shape against a mandrel with a rawhide mallet.

A textured sheet of silver formed around a bracelet mandrel.

BASIC FORMING TUTORIAL
Rings Formed from Sheet and Wire

YOU WILL NEED

- Sterling silver sheet and round wire
- Half-round pliers, parallel pliers and flat-nose pliers
- Ring and bracelet mandrels
- Rawhide mallet
- Bench vice
- Piercing saw and blade
- Flat-hand file, cut 2
- Half-round ring file, cut 2
- Tweezers
- Torch
- Soldering brick
- Pickle
- Emery paper

THE PROCESS: RING FORMED FROM SHEET

1. Anneal, cool and pickle a strip of sterling silver sheet. File the ends straight. Use half-round pliers to carefully grip one end of the strip and bend the metal to start the curve. Turn the strip and curve the opposing end in the same way.

2. Secure a ring mandrel in the bench vice and place the curved strip on it. Use a mallet to tap the strip against the mandrel, stopping partway along. To counteract the shape of the mandrel, turn the strip around and tap it in the same way to form it into a ring.

3. Tap the piece carefully with the mallet against a block of hard wood to close the form.

4. Create a tight-fitting butt join using a pair of half-round pliers. Overlap one end of the strip over the other and gently pull it back so that the ends push together under the natural springiness of the metal, forming the join.

5. Solder, cool and pickle the join. File away any solder on the inside of the seam before placing the ring on a mandrel, holding it by hand and tapping it into shape using a mallet. Turn the mandrel slowly as the ring is tapped against it. Remove the ring and turn it around to counteract the shape of the mandrel and to ensure that both edges are the same size. Repeat this turning and tapping until the ring is fully formed and perfectly round. File the outside of the join and finish the ring with emery paper.

THE PROCESS: RING FORMED FROM WIRE

6. Cut a length of round sterling silver wire longer than required and anneal, cool and pickle it. Using a mandrel secured in a bench vice, place the wire over the mandrel with one end extending slightly. Tap the wire against the mandrel with a mallet partway along its length. Then turn it around and tap it from the opposing end in the same way.

7. Tap the wire against the mandrel until the whole length has been formed around it and both ends have passed each other.

8. Use a piercing saw to cut through both wires, then place both ends together as in Step 4, without the need for filing. Solder the join, make it round and finish it as in Step 5.

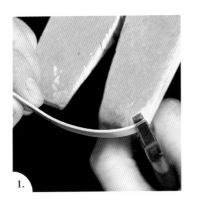

1.

2.

3.

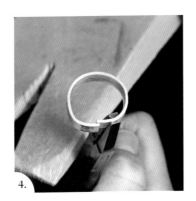

4.

7.

8.

HINTS & TIPS

Anneal the silver before forming and again once it becomes work hardened and before any further forming.

Always make rings either half or one size smaller than required to allow for the ring to become round.

When creating rings and bangles, turn the work around on the mandrel to counteract its tapered shape and to ensure that both edges become the same size.

When creating a ring from flat sheet, a butt join can be made by overlapping the ends of the strip with each other and then cutting them together with a piercing saw. This uses slightly more metal but eliminates the need for filing.

Using a flat-faced steel hammer to tap a ring against a mandrel instead of a mallet will stretch the metal. This is particularly useful to size a ring, but the hammer will thin and mark the silver, so this method should be used with care.

BASIC FORMING TUTORIAL

Bracelet Mandrel, Flat-nose Pliers, Half-round Pliers and Round-nose Pliers

YOU WILL NEED

- Hammer-textured sterling silver sheet for bangle
- Sterling silver sheet
- Round sterling silver wire
- Half-round pliers, parallel pliers and flat-nose pliers
- Bracelet mandrel
- Rawhide mallet
- Piercing saw and blades
- Flat-hand file, cut 2
- Half-round ring file, cut 2
- Tweezers
- Torch
- Soldering brick
- Pickle
- Emery paper
- Brass brush
- Pumice powder

THE PROCESS: BRACELET MANDREL

1. Hammer texture a strip of sterling silver sheet, then anneal, cool and pickle it. File both ends straight.

2. Form the strip by hand around a bracelet mandrel. Use a rawhide mallet to tap the strip against the mandrel to refine the shape.

3. Bring both ends together to create a butt join by overlapping one end of the strip over the other and gently pulling back so that the ends push together under the natural springiness of the metal. Secure the join with binding wire so that it does not come apart during soldering.

4. After soldering, file the inside of the seam to remove excess solder. Place the bangle back on the mandrel and tap it into shape using a mallet. Use this on the middle to bottom section of the bangle, keeping the mallet away from the top edge. To counteract the shape of the mandrel and to ensure that both edges became the same size, turn the piece around and repeat the tapping until the bangle is fully formed and perfectly round.

2.

4.

THE PROCESS: FLAT-NOSE PLIERS

5.   Use flat-nose pliers to create right-angled bends in a narrow strip of sterling silver sheet. Using a square and a scriber, mark a line on the strip as a guide for placing the pliers at the correct angle. Aligning the jaws of the pliers with the scribed line, grip the strip and bend the longer length up against the jaws. Use the pliers from the other side and gently squeeze to refine and square up the angle.

THE PROCESS: HALF-ROUND PLIERS

6.   Use half-round pliers to create a bezel ring from sterling silver sheet. To curve the strip and avoid damaging the silver, use the pliers with the half-round side of the jaws placed on the inside of the curve.

THE PROCESS: ROUND-NOSE PLIERS

7.   Use round-nose pliers to create a loop on the end of a round wire. After filing the end of the wire, use the very ends of the jaws to grip the wire as the pliers are turned to form the loop.

HINTS & TIPS

Heavy-gauge sheet and wire are harder to form and should be tapped over a mandrel or former using a mallet.

Silver, especially fine silver, is easily marked by pliers. Use pliers with care and take extra precautions, particularly when working with a textured surface. Use masking tape or leather on the jaws to protect the silver from marks.

Use pliers to alter and refine already-formed curves and angles, matching the jaw profile to the form to minimise any damage to the silver.

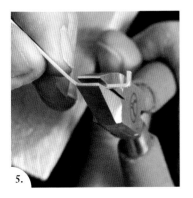

5.

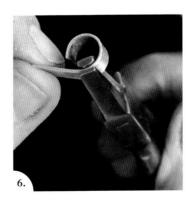

6.

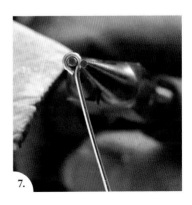

7.

SHAPING

The plasticity of silver is exploited through a range of techniques that use stakes, formers and hammers to produce three-dimensional forms for jewellery. Compared with basic forming methods, there is more scope and freedom here. Many of the techniques involve gradual change, working through various steps as forms grow. It is essential for the silver to be soft and malleable when shaping and it should be annealed regularly.

DOMING (DAPPING)

Doming (also known as dapping) involves creating a hollow dome from a disc or other shape by shallow forming using a doming block or die and a doming punch. Blocks or dies are available as cubes or rectangular blocks made from steel or brass and consist of semi-circular polished concave domes, graduating in size. Punches are made of steel or hard wood and are cylindrical, with one flat end for striking with a hammer and a rounded ball at the opposite end. They are available in sets with each rounded ball measuring a different diameter and fitting a matching concave dome on the block. Domes can be made in a variety of sizes and used in a range of ways, including creating a hollow bead by soldering two domes together. Holes made in a piece before doming takes place are likely to be stretched by the punch, so where possible holes should be made after doming. Texturing should be carried out before cutting a disc for doming: the surface will need to be protected with masking tape or by using a wooden punch. For successful doming, choose an indent on the block that is larger than the disc and a punch that is slightly smaller so that it fits in loosely: this allows for the thickness of the metal. Work down through the sizes in the block until the dome reaches the desired size and profile.

SWAGING

A swage block is a steel former with parallel grooves or channels, which, when used with the appropriate former, can create curves, troughs, and tube from flat sheet. A curved or half-round channeled swage block can be used with the cylindrical part of a doming punch or a steel rod as the former. A strip of silver is placed in the channel with the appropriate former on top. Then a mallet is used to strike the former, forcing the metal down into the channel. The trough or channel can be formed further using the block, tapping the form with a mallet and using parallel pliers to close it. For forming a tube, the piece can be pulled through a drawplate and then soldered along the seam.

SCORING AND FOLDING

This refers to the removal of metal along a line in order to fold or bend it. Once folded, the line is filled with solder to strengthen it. The removal of metal helps to create a sharp fold, whereas striking the metal over the edge of an anvil or stake without scoring first will compress the metal and the fold will be rounded. Thin sheet can be scored using a scriber, but thicker sheet should be scored with either a square needle file for narrower pieces, or a scoring tool for wider pieces. A scoring tool can be made from an old hand file by bending the end of the tang down and sharpening it. Using a steel rule as a guide and a rest for the scoring tool, the line is scored several times from the top, pulling the tool down to remove a sliver of silver. A visible raised line on the reverse side indicates that the piece is ready to bend by hand.

A curved incised line can be created by placing a piece of curved binding wire or brass, no thicker than the silver being used, on a sheet and making a single pass through the rolling mill. After annealing, the metal can be easily bent along the incised line and then soldered along the seam.

FOLD FORMING

Developed by Charles Lewton-Brain in the 1980s, fold forming utilises the properties of metal to create lightweight, strong, solder-free and flexible pieces. A bench vice, mallet, raising hammer and stake are all that is required. Silver sheet should ideally be no thicker than 26-gauge (0.4mm). Each piece starts with a fold that is shut in a bench vice and then tapped closed

with a mallet on a steel block. Alternatively, it can be pushed through a rolling mill. There are many variations for continuing from here, including opening the piece and planishing along the fold line to confirm it, or keeping the fold closed and forging with a raising or creasing hammer by striking the metal at right angles to the fold, causing the piece to curve as the metal becomes thinner. Regular annealing in-between hammering is essential. Once a sufficient curve has been achieved, the piece is annealed and prised open.

Earrings by Anne Bader.
Photo: Anne Bader.

Round silver wire shaped with pliers and then forged.

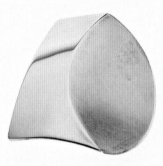

Silver sheet bent along a curved groove that was created with binding wire and a rolling mill.

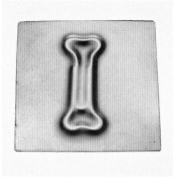
Silver sheet embossed using a paper clip.

FORGING

Forging is the controlled shaping of metal using the force of a hammer, exploiting silver's ability to stretch and elongate. It is used for spreading metal, tapering, curving and creating wedges. The type of hammer and stake or support used will directly affect the outcome – a cylindrical hammer, such as a raising or creasing hammer, will displace the metal at right angles to its curve, pushing the metal along the axis; a domed-headed hammer, such as a blocking or ball-peen hammer, will displace the metal all round. A flat stake is the most popular to work against and will not usually affect the results: a curved or rounded stake will cause the metal to spread outwards. Forged pieces can have the hammer marks left on them or these can be removed using a planishing hammer. For ease and comfort, the work should be at elbow height, with the hammer held at the end and the hammer action coming from the elbow, not the wrist. Good control of the hammer comes with practice and will result in less filing and refining of the forged shape at a later stage.

RAISING

This technique is used by silversmiths to create hollowware from a single sheet of metal without a solder seam and can be used on a small scale for creating both symmetrical and asymmetrical hollow forms for jewellery.

Silversmiths use 17–19-gauge (0.9–1.2mm) sheet, but for creating small raised forms for jewellery, 22–23-gauge (0.55–0.6mm) should suffice. Methods used for raising differ from piece to piece, but it is crucial not to work too quickly or skip stages as this may cause distortion. The first stages involve using a sandbag and either a pear-shaped mallet or a blocking hammer to create a shallow dish from a disc of silver. The next stage of raising the form involves using a raising hammer against a stake. These hammers are available in various weights with flat rectangular faces and rounded edges and corners to prevent them making deep marks in the metal. A stake is required for the hammer to form the metal. These are available in various shapes and should have a convex top profile and be rounded at the end. A stake can be made from a round steel bar or a

length of hard wood, filing and shaping the end to suit. This is an ideal way to make bespoke stakes to create smaller forms. Once the piece has been raised, the shape can be refined using a mallet against a suitable stake, such as a doming punch. The stake should match as near as possible the profile of the piece and be slightly more convex. Finally, the surface of the piece is smoothed and hardened with a planishing hammer. It is a good idea to practice with copper first to perfect your technique before working in silver.

PRESS FORMING

This technique uses pressure to push sheet metal through a hole in a die to produce three-dimensional forms. It is ideal for repeating shapes because the die can be used indefinitely. The process can also be used to emboss silver where the metal is formed over an object: for this to work, the object should be free from undercuts and must be strong enough to survive the pressure involved. Silver is very well suited to press forming using 20–24-gauge (0.5–0.8mm) sheet. Fine and Britannia silver are easier to form than sterling. The silver can be textured beforehand, although a little distortion may occur during the press-forming process.

The pressure needed for this technique comes from using either a bench vice, fly press or hydraulic press. Using a bench vice limits the amount of pressure that is possible, making it only suitable for use with small dies and thinner sheet. A hydraulic press is more powerful and is easier to use, allowing larger pieces to be pressed from thicker sheet. Dies can be made by cutting a shape from 1cm (⅜in) acrylic sheet. If many forms are going to be created from the same die, it must be strengthened by attaching a sheet of brass with a matching shape cut from it. Organic shapes are better suited for this technique and shapes with corners should be avoided.

An annealed sheet of silver is taped down over the die and a rubber sheet placed on top: steel plates or blocks placed either side are used to distribute the pressure. The forming may take several pressings to reach the desired depth and the silver will need to be removed and annealed. Once formed, the shape can be cut from the sheet and used in many different ways, such as soldering two identical forms together or working the forms further using techniques such as chasing.

Reversible necklace by Elizabeth Bone. Photo: Joel Degen.

SHAPING TUTORIAL
Doming and Swaging

YOU WILL NEED
FOR DOMING
- Sterling silver sheet
- Disc template/dividers
- Scriber
- Piercing saw
- Hand file
- Doming block
- Doming punches
- Mallet
- Torch
- Fire brick
- Tweezers
- Pickle

FOR SWAGING
- Silver sheet
- Swage block
- Hand file
- Doming punches and/or steel rod for formers
- Mallet
- Torch
- Fire brick
- Tweezers
- Pickle

THE PROCESS: DOMING

1. Mark a circle on a silver sheet using a template and a scriber. Cut out the circle using a piercing saw and file around the edge with a flat-hand file to refine the shape. Then anneal, cool and pickle the disc.

2. Choose an indent in the doming block that has a larger diameter than the disc and place the disc in centrally. Choose a punch that is slightly smaller than the indent and fit it in loosely. Place the punch on top of the silver disc and hit it several times with the mallet, using powerful blows to force the metal down.

3. Working down through the different-sized indents in the block and changing the punch where necessary, form the dome further until the desired size and profile is reached.

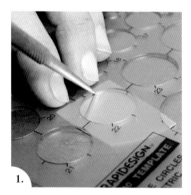

1.

2.

3.

THE PROCESS: SWAGING

4.   Cut and anneal a strip of sterling silver sheet, then place it in a channel on the swage block. Place a doming punch that fits the channel over the silver sheet to use as a former.

5.   Use a mallet to tap the punch down into the channel and form the silver into an even curve. Repeat this in the next channel using a smaller former.

6.   Straighten and even the edges using a cut 2 flat-hand file.

7.   Working on a wooden surface, carefully tap the edges with a mallet to bring them together. Gently squeeze the join with a pair of parallel pliers to close it ready for soldering.

4.

5.

6.

7.

HINTS & TIPS

Texturing the silver should be carried out before cutting a disc for doming.

A textured surface needs to be protected with masking tape before doming. You can also use a wooden punch instead of a steel one.

Don't force a disc into an indent on the block where it doesn't fit properly. Start forming a dome in a larger indent and gradually reduce it until the dome reaches the desired size and profile. If this is not done, the metal can crinkle at the top edge.

Doming and swaging both require the silver to be annealed regularly.

A swage block can be used to form curves and troughs from longer strips of metal, or the curved forms can have their edges closed and soldered to create tube.

Tube can be formed by cutting through the swaged form with a piercing saw once the edges have been brought together; these edges are then tapped together with a mallet on a wooden block and soldered.

SHAPING TUTORIAL

Scoring and Folding by Michael Milloy

YOU WILL NEED

- Silver sheet and rectangular wire
- Scriber
- Square
- Dividers (optional)
- Steel rule
- Block of wood
- Nails and jobbing hammer
- C (G) clamp
- Square needle file, cut 2
- Steel binding wire
- Scoring tool
- Torch
- Tweezers
- Fire brick
- Solder
- Pickle

THE PROCESS: SCORING

1. To create a backstop, hammer two nails into a block of wood towards one end. Clamp the wood securely to the workbench.

2. Mark two lines on the silver sheet with a marker pen. Place a steel rule along each line and use a scriber several times to scribe a deep line.

3. Place the silver sheet on the wooden block with its bottom edge firmly against the nails. With the steel rule positioned against the scribed line acting as a guide, place the scoring tool at the top edge with its point located in the groove created by the scriber; pull it firmly towards the nails. Repeat this several times; each time a sliver of metal will be removed from the groove. Remove the steel rule once the groove is deep enough and the scoring tool is able to travel down without the aid of a guide.

4. Stop the scoring when a raised line starts to appear on the reverse side of the sheet. Use a square file to refine the scored line.

5. Bend the sheet along the scored line by hand. Clean with pumice powder and a brass brush, then stick-feed solder the fold line with hard silver solder.

6. Using a square and scriber, mark perpendicular lines at regular intervals along a rectangular piece of sterling silver wire. With the wire held firmly against the bench peg, use a square needle file at a slight angle to file a notch. Gradually file the notch into a V-shape across the width of the wire. Turn the strip and repeat the filing from the other side, stopping when the notch is three quarters through the wire.

7. Bend the wire using your fingers and flat-nose pliers. After cleaning, chip/pallion solder the fold line with hard silver solder.

THE PROCESS: FOLDING

8. Anneal and curve a piece of steel binding wire around a mandrel. Position the wire on a piece of annealed silver sheet and pass them once through the rolling mill together using firm pressure.

9. Anneal and pickle the silver and bend the sheet by hand along the curved groove. After cleaning, solder the fold line.

3.

4.

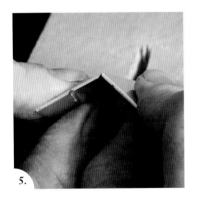
5.

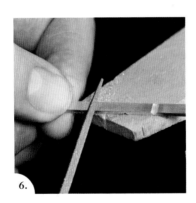
6.

7.

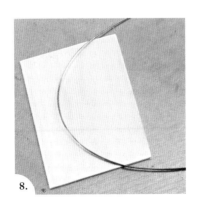
8.

HINTS & TIPS

Thin sheet should be scored using a scriber instead of a scoring tool.

When using a steel rule as a guide for the scoring tool, clamp it down to prevent it from moving around.

It is better to score lightly many times over than to use too much pressure to try to complete the job in only one or two attempts.

Make sure that the scoring does not go too far through the silver as this may cause it to split when it is bent. Stop scoring when a raised line appears on the reverse side.

Wire used to create an incised line with the rolling mill should not be thicker than the silver being formed.

When using a scoring tool, the silver sheet should ideally be no thinner than 18-gauge (1mm).

SHAPING TUTORIAL
Fold Forming

YOU WILL NEED

- 26-gauge (0.4mm) sterling silver sheet
- Bench vice
- Mallet
- Raising or creasing hammer
- Bench anvil
- Steel block
- Torch
- Fire brick
- Tweezers
- Pickle

THE PROCESS

1. Cut and anneal a rectangle of 26-gauge (0.4mm) silver sheet. Fold the strip in half lengthways and place it in a bench vice with protective jaws to squeeze the fold together. Tap the fold closed with a mallet on a steel block.

2. With the fold on the left, draw a curve to the right of the fold with a marker pen and use tin snips to cut along the curve. Use a flat-hand file to neaten the edge.

3. Mark a centre line and two arrows on the piece to indicate the position and the directions from which the forging will take place.

4. Forge the piece on an anvil using the narrower end of a raising hammer at right angles to the fold. Starting in the centre and travelling upwards and then downwards from the centre, overlap the hammer marks, keeping the blows away from the folded edge. Repeat the forging process on the reverse side in exactly the same way. Anneal the piece and leave it to cool on a steel block.

5. Continue the forging process in exactly the same way as Step 4, working both sides with the hammer in two opposing directions from the centre: then anneal the piece and leave it to cool on a steel block. The metal will gradually begin to curve as the forging causes it to become thinner in one area.

6. Repeat the process until the desired curve has been achieved, making sure that the forging stops before the silver becomes too thin. Finally, anneal, cool and pickle the piece. Prise the form open using a wooden chopstick, then shape and twist it by hand to offset the ends.

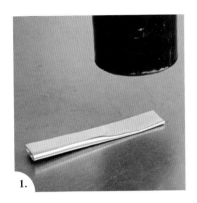

1.

2.

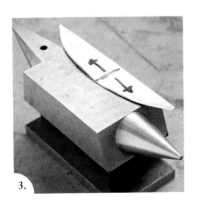

3.

4.

5.

6.

HINTS & TIPS

Keep the hammer blows away from the very edge of the fold.

Do not pickle after annealing: let the piece cool on a steel block before continuing with the forging.

As the curve starts to form, the piece will need to be flattened with a mallet after annealing and before forging.

Make sure the silver does not become too thin or it may split.

An alternative way to create this form is to insert a narrow strip of 18-gauge (1mm) copper sheet into the fold before placing it in the bench vice and then tapping it closed. Proceed in the same way as Step 2 to cut a curve. After annealing, feed the piece through a rolling mill with the fold at a right angle to the rollers. Continue like this, annealing regularly, keeping the same angle with the rollers and readjusting if necessary as the curve develops. Once the folded side has become the same thickness as the rest of the sheet and the curve has formed, anneal and open the form removing the copper.

SHAPING TUTORIAL
Forging

YOU WILL NEED

- Round sterling silver rod
- Raising hammer
- Steel block
- Curved stake
- Bench vice
- Round mandrel
- Torch
- Fire brick
- Tweezers
- Pickle
- Files
- Emery paper

THE PROCESS

1. Using a raising hammer and working against a flat steel block, flatten an annealed piece of round silver rod along one side. Starting partway down the rod, use the hammer to strike the rod at right angles delivering regular, even blows to create hammer marks that overlap each other. Work all four sides in the same way, turning the rod 90° each time. Anneal and pickle the rod.

2. Create a taper by working on the bottom 2cm (¾in) of the rod in the same way as Step 1, turning it 90° each time and using regular and even overlapping hammer blows along all four sides, gradually reducing the area that is worked towards the end of the rod. Then anneal and pickle the rod.

3. To form a round section from the tapered rod, use a raising hammer to flatten the corners creating eight sides. Then anneal and pickle the rod.

4. Use a planishing hammer to round the taper. Slowly turn the rod as the hammer planishes and refines it. Then paper the rod.

5. Anneal and form a piece of round silver rod around a mandrel. Working on a curved stake secured in a bench vice, use a raising hammer to spread the metal at the curve. Apply regular and even overlapping hammer blows at right angles to the curve. Anneal the piece regularly. Use a planishing hammer to refine and remove the hammer marks and finish the piece with emery paper.

6. Anneal and form a piece of round silver rod with half-round pliers. Working on a curved stake secured in a bench vice, use a raising hammer to spread the metal in one area. Apply regular and even overlapping hammer blows at right angles to the curve. Anneal the piece regularly. Use a planishing hammer to refine and remove the hammer marks and finish the piece with emery paper.

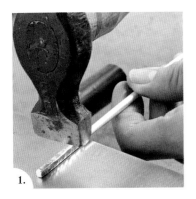

1.

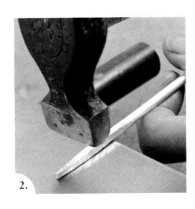

2.

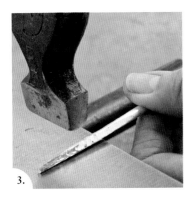

3.

4.

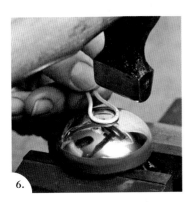

6.

HINTS & TIPS

Hammer faces should be polished and stakes kept in good condition, any marks on them will transfer to the metal.

Ear protection may be necessary during forging.

Work on a sturdy flat surface. Make sure stakes are well secured in the vice before commencing work.

For ease and comfort, the work should be at the same height as your elbow, with the hammer held at the end and the hammer action coming from your elbow and not your wrist.

Uneven hammer blows applied when forging a square section from a round rod will cause the taper to become a rhombus. Check the shape regularly and either file to correct it, or forge it to a round rod before re-establishing the square section.

SHAPING TUTORIAL

Raising by Adaesi Ukairo

YOU WILL NEED

- Fine silver sheet
- Dividers
- Piercing saw
- Pencil and compasses (optional)
- Sandbag
- Blocking hammer
- Raising hammer
- Planishing hammer
- Rawhide mallet
- Stake
- Bench vice
- Doming punch
- Torch
- Tweezers
- Pickle

THE PROCESS

1. Scribe a 72mm (2¾in) circle on a fine silver sheet using dividers. Cut the disc out using a piercing saw, file the edges and anneal the piece. Scribe a 3cm (1³⁄₁₆in) circle on the disc, followed by two further circles at 7mm (⁴⁄₁₆in) intervals.

2. To hollow the disc, place it on a sandbag with the scribed circles face down. Working from the outside edge into the centre, use a blocking hammer to strike the metal. Hold the hammer in a fixed striking position while the disc is turned and directed inwards in a circular pattern. To prevent the edge of the metal cutting into the sandbag, transfer the piece to a block of wood and continue hammering to the edge. Repeat this process until a shallow dish has formed, annealing when necessary.

3. To raise the shallow dish, anneal and work it from the other side against a curved stake, secured in a bench vice, using a raising hammer. Hold the dish with the working area in contact with the front top area of the stake. Starting between the first and second circles, use the hammer to create overlapping marks as it lays the silver against the stake, with each blow making a distinct step in the metal. While the piece is hammered, slowly turn it in a clockwise direction. Carry out this circular hammering from the first circle in the centre, stopping just before the top edge where a mallet is used instead of the raising hammer.

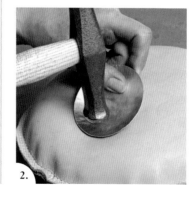

2.

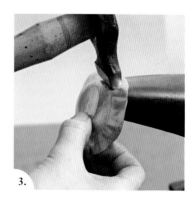

3.

4. After each course of raising, anneal the silver and redraw the circles if necessary. Repeat the raising until the sides come in. Use a mallet to form the top edge and hammer out any pleats that start to form.

5. Place the piece on a sandbag and use a blocking hammer to dome out the bottom.

6. To decrease the diameter at the top, place the piece back on the stake and use the raising hammer to take in the sides of the form. Starting at a point halfway up side of the piece, use the hammer to deliver overlapping blows working around the piece as in Step 3. After each course of raising and annealing, reposition the starting point above the last, gradually moving it towards the top of the piece. Use the mallet at the top edge each time.

7. Carry out final shaping using a mallet and a suitable sized doming punch secured in the bench vice. Place the hollow form over the punch and use the mallet to refine and smooth the shape.

8. Finally, use a planishing hammer to remove any marks made by the raising hammer and smooth the surface of the silver. Place the hollow form over the doming punch and planish from the centre to the outside edge while turning the work.

HINTS & TIPS

Cracks can be repaired with hard silver solder.

Unless an asymmetric form is required, always work from an accurate centre using circles as a guide.

A pear-shaped mallet can be used for hollowing instead of a blocking hammer.

Don't hammer the top edge against a sandbag as this will eventually cause the bag to split. Use an old tree trunk or block of wood with a hollow carved out of it.

Raising too fast will create pleats around the top. These can be removed using a mallet.

4.

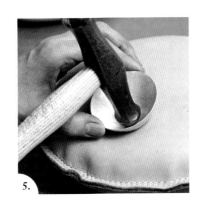

5.

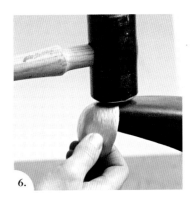

6.

SHAPING TUTORIAL
Press Forming and Embossing

YOU WILL NEED

- Piece of 23-gauge (0.55mm) Britannia or fine silver sheet
- 1cm (⅜in) thick acrylic sheet
- Marker pen
- Drill bit and bench drill
- Piercing saw and blades
- Half-round hand file
- Rubber sheet
- Craft knife
- Masking tape
- Suitable object for embossing
- Torch
- Fire brick
- Tweezers
- Pickle
- Hydraulic or fly press

THE PROCESS: PRESS FORMING

1. Draw a shape on to a piece of acrylic sheet with a marker pen and drill a small access hole just inside the shape. Use a piercing saw to cut out the shape, keeping the blade vertical throughout. Refine the shape using a half-round hand file, keeping the edges crisp.

2. Cut the silver sheet approximately 1cm (⅜in) larger than the cutout and anneal it. Place it over the acrylic die, centreing it over the cutout shape and secure it with masking tape, then place a sheet of rubber on top. Set this on a steel block in the press and place a second steel block on top of the rubber. Use the press to apply pressure; the steel blocks help to distribute this pressure evenly (when using a hydraulic press, increase the pressure to raise the shelf and release the pressure when resistance is met).

3. Remove the stack from the press to check the forming progress. Cut a piece of rubber sheet to fit the newly-formed indent and place the sheet into the indent. Replace the rubber sheet on top and return the stack to the press for further forming as in Step 2.

4. After removing and checking the progress of the forming, anneal the silver and then return it to the die. Place a slightly smaller piece of rubber sheet in the indent and carry out further forming. Repeat this process until a deep enough depression has been created.

THE PROCESS: EMBOSSING

5. Place your chosen object on a steel block, then place a sheet of annealed silver centrally over it, securing it with masking tape.

6. Place the piece in the press with a rubber sheet on top of the silver and a steel block on top of the rubber. Use the press to apply pressure (when using a hydraulic press increase the pressure to raise the shelf, release the pressure when resistance is met). Repeat this, annealing regularly until the embossed shape has formed in the silver.

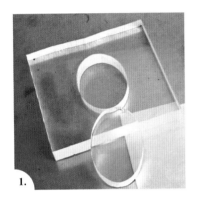

1.

2.

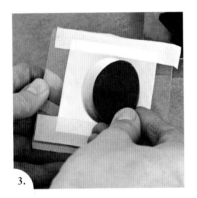

3.

4.

5.

6.

HINTS & TIPS

Use a thicker saw blade or a wax saw blade for piercing the acrylic.

For deeper forms, use a hydraulic press and a thicker sheet of silver. Increase the depth of the die by using two sheets of acrylic together.

To strengthen a die and increase its life, attach a sheet of brass with a matching shape cut from it.

Press forming should be done in stages – too much pressure at one time will cause the silver to split. Anneal regularly.

Remove wrinkles that may form in the silver around the edges with a mallet on a steel block, taking care not to hit the formed shape.

Objects used for embossing should be strong enough to survive the pressure involved.

Ring by Anne Bader. Photo: Anne Bader.

Sterling silver wire-wrapped ring by Jessica Rose.

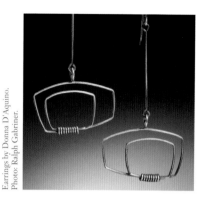

Earrings by Donna D'Aquino. Photo: Ralph Gabriner.

COLD CONNECTIONS

Cold connections provide ways of joining that do not involve heat and soldering. They are useful when joining different materials to silver or when incorporating a material into a piece of jewellery that will not withstand heat. They can be purely functional, such as a hinge, but they can also combine function and decoration together.

WIRE WRAPPING

This technique can effectively hold and support almost any shape or material. It also works equally successfully on its own, where the wire wraps and binds around itself to create three-dimensional pieces.

Sterling-silver wire with a round, square or half-round profile is suitable for wire wrapping. Half-round wire is a good choice for wrapping a wire bundle and also provides comfort during wearing for wire-wrapped pieces such as rings. A thinner gauge wire offers more flexibility and is easier to use, whereas a thicker gauge is more

difficult to manipulate and the results are not as neat. Soft wire is easier to bend, but any mistakes are difficult to rectify, often leaving the wire kinked. Soft wire is also easily marked by tools, so is best used for twisting. Half-hard wire is more forgiving and holds its shape well.

20-gauge (0.8mm) is an ideal size to use for half-hard wire and 18-gauge (1.0mm) for half-round wire. 24-gauge (0.6mm) and 28-gauge (0.4mm) are suitable for twisting to create decorative wires and binding. Thinner wires can be bound together to provide enough strength and support to hold an object.

The basic techniques used to create wire-wrapped pieces are twisting, wrapping bundles of wire, bending and shaping. Wire wrapping is a very accessible technique; most of the work can be carried out using a simple set of tools, including pliers, wire cutters, a pin vice, a steel block, a mallet and a needle file. Planning and practice are key; work out your design using copper wire first before moving on to silver.

RIVETING

Rivets are pins made from wire or tube. A basic rivet is a pin with a head; the shank of the pin is passed through a hole in the parts to be joined, and a rivet head is created on the second end by spreading the metal with a hammer.

Rivets can be used to hold two or more components together tightly, to create a gap between parts using spacers made from tube, to allow movement or to join parts together where the use of heat for soldering would weaken a crucial part. Sterling silver wire or tube is suitable for rivets: wire should be half-hard or work hardened before use.

A riveted join that pivots is made by placing a piece of paper in between the parts being joined. After forming the rivet, the paper is removed by burning or soaking it in water.

Rivet heads can sit on the surface of the metal or they can be countersunk. A countersunk hole is made by enlarging the opening of the drilled hole on one or both sides with a bud or ball burr in a pendant motor. This creates a space where the spread of the rivet head can sit below the surface. There are several ways to form rivet heads before the rivet is used, including spreading the metal at one end of a wire with a hammer; melting a ball on the end of a wire, then shaping it by hammering it in a drawplate and filing; and soldering a wire on to a piece of textured silver. The last two methods are useful for making a decorative feature of the rivet and also for when a larger head is required. Creating rivet heads on tube can be achieved without directly hammering the piece, which is useful for pieces where hammering would damage the parts being joined.

For successful riveting, first finish all the parts to be joined. Make sure that holes are drilled at exactly the same diameter as the wire or tube. Drill and countersink all the holes in one part first (this could be the top piece), put the pieces together and make a mark through one hole on to the piece underneath. Drill this hole and rivet the parts together through this. Drill a second hole and rivet that, then drill all the other holes and finish the riveting.

Dark Hydra brooch by Wendy McAllister. Photo: Hap Sakwa.

COLD CONNECTIONS TUTORIAL

Wire Wrapping by Jessica Rose

YOU WILL NEED

- 18-gauge (1.0mm) sterling silver square wire
- 18-gauge (1.0mm) half-round wire
- Stone (picture jasper was used here)
- Beading mat
- Snipe-nose pliers
- Round-nose pliers
- Wire cutters
- Tape measure
- Needle file
- Two pin vices
- Masking tape
- Marker pen
- Bench vice

THE PROCESS

1. Straighten the wires by securing one end in a bench vice and giving several sharp tugs from the other end using pliers. Cut two pieces of square wire, each long enough to wrap twice around the stone, and two pieces 5cm (2in) longer. Twist each of the longer wires separately using the pin vices.

2. Cut a 15cm (5¹⁴⁄₁₆in) length of half-round wire. File one end flat and bend it using round-nose pliers into a U-shape, with the flat part on the inside.

3. Place the two lengths of twisted square wire together, with one length of square wire on either side: secure them with masking tape at the ends. Mark the centre with a marker pen and hook the half-round wire on at this point. Use pliers to gently squeeze the hook closed against the bundle of wires. With the pliers still gripping the hook, make several wraps with the wire by hand, pulling the wire tightly around the bundle, making sure that on one side the wire is at right angles to the others and that each wire lies next to the other without a gap. Use the pliers to press the wrap in place and neaten it.

4. Cut the wire so that both cut ends are on the same side – the side that will become the inside of the wrap. File them smooth and squeeze them back down with the snipe-nose pliers.

5. Shape the length of wrapped wires around the stone, forming it by hand. Mark two points along the wires with marker pen on the left and right sides, both equal distance from the wrap.

6. Cut two 10cm (4in) lengths of half-round wire and prepare one end of each, as in Step 2. Hook one piece of the half-round wire on to the bundle of wire at one of the marks. Make several wraps. Repeat this on the opposite side of the bundle at the mark.

7. Place the stone inside the bundle and cross the wires over each other at the top. Highlight the point where they cross with marker pen.

8. Make a small bend on one side of the bundle with snipe-nose pliers, using the mark made in Step 5 as a guide. Take a measurement from one of the last formed wraps to the point of the bend. Measure this distance and mark it on the opposite side and bend the wires in the same way.

9. Place the stone inside the wire frame to check the fit. Use a length of the half-round wire, make several wraps to hold all the wires together at the top, just above the point where the bends have formed. This secures the frame.

10. To support the stone from behind, pull the square wire on the back of the frame at the same point on the left- and right-sides using snipe-nose pliers.

11. To secure the stone in the frame, pull the square-frame wire in on the front of the piece out over the stone at different points on the left and right sides.

12. To create a fitting, twist the four untwisted square wires left from the frame construction using a pin vice. Coil one twisted wire into a spiral and position it over the stone. Leave one twisted wire long, and cut the remainder to 12–14mm (⁷⁄₁₆–⁹⁄₁₆in) long. Curl these wires down using round-nose pliers. Form a bail from the long twisted wire using round-nose pliers, then wrap the end around and cut.

HINTS & TIPS

Make sure that square wire is straight before working with it.

Manipulating wire will work harden it. Too much reworking of a piece causes it to become brittle and eventually break.

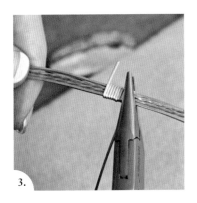
3.

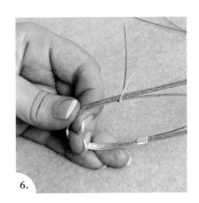
6.

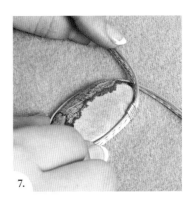
7.

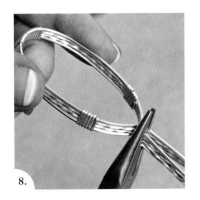
8.

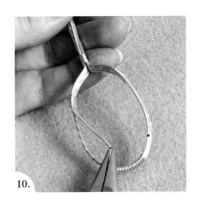
10.

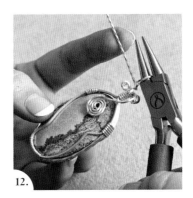
12.

COLD CONNECTIONS TUTORIAL

Rivets

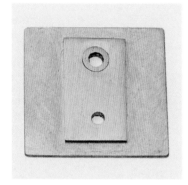

YOU WILL NEED

- Sterling silver sheet in various sizes for joining
- Gold wire, tube
- Micrometre or vernier gauge
- Ruler
- Marker pen
- Drill bits at the same diameter as the wire and tube
- Centre punch
- Jobbing hammer
- Bud or ball burr
- Pendant motor
- Drawplate
- Bench vice
- Steel block
- Planishing hammer
- Small ball-peen hammer
- Doming punches
- Burnisher
- Wire and tube cutters
- Snipe-nose and flat-nose pliers
- Piercing saw and blades
- Flat needle and hand file
- Emery paper
- Masking tape

THE PROCESS

1. Secure a length of round gold wire in the protective jaws of the bench vice. File the end flat and then tap it with a ball-peen hammer to spread the metal and create a rivet head.

2. Mark the position of the rivets on the uppermost part being joined and make the holes using a drill bit with the same diameter as the rivet wire. Tape together the two parts to be joined and drill one hole through to the second sheet.

3. Use a bud or ball burr mounted in a pendant motor to countersink the hole on both sides by widening the opening of the hole.

4. Push the rivet through the hole and cut off the excess with wire cutters, leaving enough to file the end flat and form the rivet head.

5. Working on a flat steel block, tap the end of the wire with a ball-peen hammer to spread the metal and form the rivet head.

6. Use a flat needle file to file down any metal sitting on the surface, then use an emery stick to remove the file marks.

7. Form rivet heads by melting a ball on the end of a wire. Using a drawplate clamped in a bench vice, place the balled wire in a hole of the same diameter and use a planishing hammer to flatten the ball.

8. File the flattened ends into shapes and prepare the parts being joined as in Step 2. Countersink the hole very slightly on the front to create a space for any unevenness where the wire and the shape meet. Push the rivet through the hole and cut the excess off at the back with wire cutters, leaving enough to file the end flat and form the rivet head.

9. Working on a flat steel block with a piece of paper on top to protect the already-formed rivet head, tap the end of the wire with a ball-peen hammer to spread the metal and form the rivet head, as in Step 5.

10. Cut a short length of tube using a tube cutter and piercing saw. Prepare the parts being joined as in Step 2 and countersink the holes as in Step 3. After annealing the tube, insert it into the hole and use a burnisher to spread out one end of the tube. Tap the rivet head down against a steel block using a small doming punch.

1.

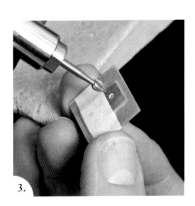

3.

5.

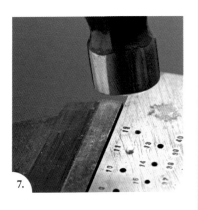

7.

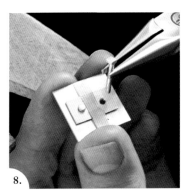

8.

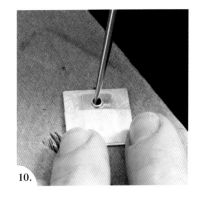

10.

HINTS & TIPS

Finish all parts before riveting them together.

The rivet should fit tightly in the hole. Use a drill bit that's the same diameter as the shank of the rivet.

When forming the rivet head with a hammer, try not to hit the surface of the metal being joined. You can use masking tape to protect the surface.

Protect decorative rivet heads when forming the head on the reverse side by using paper or leather on a steel block.

It is easier to pre-form one end of a piece of tube with a burnisher before the tube is cut.

WIREWORK AND CHAINS

WIRE

Wire is a versatile material that is available in a wide range of sizes and shapes. It can be used alone or in combination with other silver materials, as well as with stones and beads. Wire is easily manipulated using twisting, wrapping, coiling and binding techniques, making it perfect for cold connections and creating decorative details. In addition to this, using heat to melt a ball on the end of a wire is a useful way to form rivet heads.

Wire is available as sterling, fine and Argentium silver in a number of different profiles and sizes, including round, square, rectangular, triangular, oval, half-round and patterned. Round is the most popular and is supplied in a range of sizes from a fine 32-gauge (0.2mm) up to a 2-gauge (6mm). Anything larger than this is usually described as rod. Sterling silver wire is generally sold as soft, but there may be some exceptions, depending on where it is purchased. Round sterling silver wire is available as hard, half-hard and soft. Solder-filled round wire is available in a limited number of sizes and is ideal for creating chains and jump rings. Only flux is required, which helps to speed up the soldering process.

Wire is ductile, meaning it's capable of being drawn out with the use of a drawplate. A drawplate is a die with numbered holes of any shape that are graded in size and used to reduce the size of wire, change its shape or harden it by passing the wire through the same hole several times. A drawplate is a useful tool because it allows you to quickly make a different size and/or shape of wire from an existing one. Some rolling mills have half-round and square wire grooves that work in a similar way to a drawplate.

Wire is usually supplied on a reel or as a coil and often needs to be straightened out before it can be used. This can be done by securing one end in a bench vice and using pliers to hold the other end of the wire while pulling it taut several times. Work hardening wire parts during the making or after completion of a piece may be necessary, especially if fine silver has been used. This can be carried out against a steel block using a planishing hammer or with a burnisher. If these options are not possible, work hardening can also be done in a barrel polisher.

CHAINS

A chain is a series of connecting or interlocking units that articulate when put together. Although traditionally made from wire links or jump rings, chain can also be created from other units that can be made up of repeated or random forms. The chain must be flexible and comfortable to wear.

Chains made to suspend a pendant from are usually designed to complement the piece and are often understated so that they do not distract from the focal point of the pendant. They should be strong enough to support a suspended piece and be able to withstand wear and tear without distorting or breaking.

Mandrels, formers, pliers, a piercing saw, hammers, a steel block and soldering equipment are all required for chain making. Mandrels can be created from items such as drill bits, knitting needles and steel rod. Many different profile wires can be used to create chain, but round wire works particularly well with 18-gauge (1mm) being a good choice. Varying the size of links, using a different-shaped wire, twisting, texturing with a hammer or flattening jump rings through a rolling mill are all techniques that can be used to create links. In order for a chain to sit and hang properly, avoid having longer links in the sections that sit around the neck and at the opposite end where the chain curves around.

Fusing links together instead of soldering is a quicker and more efficient way of working. Argentium silver can be used very successfully for fusing; it's worth spending time practising to gain confidence with this technique. Some chain, such as

chain mail, can be constructed without soldering or fusing, in which case a heavier gauge wire should be used.

Chain should never be polished on a polishing machine; polishing threads, a brass brush with soap or a barrel polisher should be used instead.

Broken Borders necklace by Sun-Woong Bang. Photo: Grant Hancock.

WIREWORK TUTORIAL
Drawing Wire Down and Making Jump Rings

YOU WILL NEED

- Round and square silver wire in various sizes
- Drawplate
- Bench vice
- Draw tongs
- Beeswax
- Hand and needle files
- Mandrel
- Piercing saw and blades
- Hand drill (wheel brace)
- Serrated, flat, round, parallel and snipe-nose pliers
- Hide mallet
- Tweezers
- Reverse-action tweezers
- Soldering probe
- Hard silver solder
- Torch
- Soldering brick/charcoal block
- Pickle
- Planishing hammer
- Steel block
- Rolling mills (optional)
- Hole and peg jig or piece of wood and headless nails or pins
- Barrel polisher (optional)

THE PROCESS: DRAWING WIRE DOWN

1. Before working with some wires, it may be necessary to straighten them by securing one end in the jaws of a bench vice while holding the other end in a pair of serrated pliers, and then giving the wire a short, sharp tug.

2. Anneal, quench and pickle a length of sterling silver wire. File one end of the wire to a taper, so that when it is inserted into the drawplate hole there is sufficient wire extending through the hole for the draw tongs to grip. Apply beeswax to the wire to help pull it smoothly through the hole.

3. Secure the drawplate in a bench vice and insert the tapered end of the wire into the holes from the back of the drawplate. When a hole is found that the wire does not fit through easily, use the draw tongs to grip the tapered end tightly and pull the wire through. Draw the wire down hole by hole, annealing it after every two or three holes, until the desired size has been reached.

3.

4.

THE PROCESS: MAKING JUMP RINGS

4.   Anneal and pickle a length of round silver wire, then wrap it once around a steel mandrel. Secure the mandrel in a bench vice, trapping the wrapped wire between the jaws of the vice and the mandrel. Wrap the wire tightly around the mandrel.

5.   Remove the coil from the mandrel and cut the rings off using a piercing saw. Working against a bench peg for support, use the saw at a slight angle to cut down one side of the coil so that the rings drop off one by one.

6.   Close the jump rings using two pairs of flat-nose pliers and clean the join area with Scotch-Brite. Place the rings together on a charcoal block: flux and solder them using a small pallion of hard silver solder for each one. After pickling, rinsing and drying, clean up any excess solder with a needle file and then emery paper.

5.

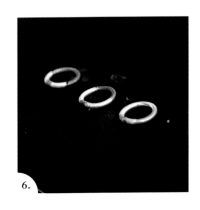

6.

WIREWORK TUTORIAL

Twisting Wire, Making a Spiral, Making Decorative Wire and Making Repeated Wire Components Using a Jig

THE PROCESS: TWISTING WIRE

7.   Anneal, quench and pickle a length of square sterling silver wire. Secure one end in the jaws of a bench vice and the other end in the chuck of a hand drill (wheel brace). With the wire held taut, turn the handle of the drill slowly until the desired twist in the wire is created. Anneal the wire.

THE PROCESS: MAKING A SPIRAL

8.   Anneal, quench and pickle a length of plain or twisted wire. To start the spiral, use the smallest part of a pair of round-nose pliers to grip the very end of the wire and wrap it once around the pliers.

9.   To form the rest of the spiral, use flat-nose pliers to hold the piece firmly, while your free hand pulls the wire around and against the curve of the forming spiral. Move the position of the flat-nose pliers as the spiral grows.

7.

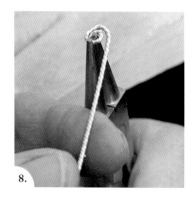

8.

10.

THE PROCESS: MAKING DECORATIVE WIRE

10. Bend a length of round sterling silver wire in half, forming a loop in the middle. Secure the two ends in a bench vice and attach the loop to a hook that has been secured in the chuck of a hand drill (wheel brace). With the wire held taut, slowly turn the handle of the drill until the desired twist in the wire is achieved. Loosely coil the wire and anneal it. Flatten a short length of the twisted wire against a flat plate, applying regular blows along its length with a planishing hammer.

THE PROCESS: MAKING REPEATED WIRE COMPONENTS USING A JIG

11. Use a hole and peg jig to create repeated wire shapes from an annealed round sterling silver wire. Work out a design on paper, then use the pegs set in the jig to create the design. Using a longer length of wire than required, form a loop on one end with round-nose pliers. Place the loop over one of the pegs and wrap the wire tightly around them. Note the direction the wire took so that repeats of the design can be made.

12. Before the shape is removed from the jig, pull the wire tight using parallel pliers. Once removed, cut the wire with a piercing saw and use pliers for any necessary shape refining before barrel polishing.

HINTS & TIPS

Use soft or half-hard wire for forming, or anneal wires before any forming takes place. Twisted wires should be annealed before they are used.

Several wires can be twisted together, including different profiled wires. Stop twisting as soon as the desired twist has been achieved. Two pin vices can be used instead of a hand drill (wheel brace).

Cut twisted wires on the diagonal, rather than the straight, to help prevent them untwisting.

A simple jig can be made with a piece of wood and headless nails or pins.

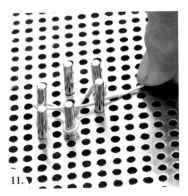

11.

12.

CHAIN TUTORIAL
Basic Chain and Flattened Oval Link Chain

YOU WILL NEED

- Round sterling silver wire
- Various-sized mandrels
- Bench vice
- Piercing saw and blades
- Scribers
- Hand file
- Needle files
- Emery paper
- Flat, parallel, round and snipe-nose pliers
- Hide mallet
- Hard and medium silver solder
- Tweezers
- Torch
- Soldering brick or charcoal block
- Pickle
- Planishing hammer
- Steel block
- Rolling mills
- Brass brush, soap and pumice powder
- Barrel polisher

THE PROCESS: BASIC CHAIN

1. To create a basic chain, make jump rings from round sterling silver wire using a steel mandrel. Close half the jump rings and solder them with hard silver solder.

2. Join groups of three rings by using one unsoldered jump ring to join two soldered links. Use two pairs of flat-nose pliers to close the jump ring.

3. Using one small pallion of hard silver solder, solder the ring with its join positioned away from the other rings.

4. Link the groups of three rings to each other in the same way as Steps 2 and 3 until all the links are joined to form the chain. Attach a suitable catch to the chain and clean any joins that require it with a file and then emery paper. Barrel polish the completed chain for about an hour or until sufficiently polished.

2.

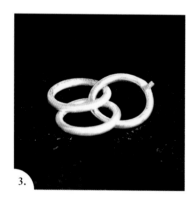

3.

THE PROCESS: FLATTENED OVAL LINK CHAIN

5. Make large jump rings on a mandrel. Close and solder all the rings. After cleaning up the joins, pass each individual ring through the rolling mill several times until a flattened oval shape is created. Locate the solder join on half of the ovals by gently heating them with a soft flame until a dark line or discoloured area shows. Cool the pieces on a steel block, then use a piercing saw with a fine blade to cut the joins open carefully.

6. Use one cut oval link to join two soldered oval links together and resolder the cut link to make the join. Continue to create the chain in this way until the desired length is achieved.

HINTS & TIPS

Using a different profile of wire and varying the size and/ or shape of the link will create a more interesting chain.

Chains should be comfortable to wear, flexible and strong enough to withstand wear and tear.

Where there are lots of jump rings, solder as many as possible in one go. Lay them out on a soldering brick so they are fairly close together, but not touching. Flux each join and place a small pallion of solder on, then heat each one and run the solder. The heat from one will transfer to the next, making the whole process a little quicker.

Fusing links together can be quicker than soldering.

Work harden components where necessary against a steel block using a planishing hammer. Where this is not possible, work harden using a barrel polisher.

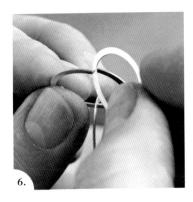

5.

6.

CHAIN TUTORIAL

Ball-and-loop Link and Sailor's Chain

THE PROCESS: BALL-AND-LOOP LINK

7. Create a simple linking system, not based on jump rings, using a ball-and-loop method. Cut a number of wires longer than required for your piece and melt a ball on one end. Hold a sterling silver wire in reverse-action tweezers and dip one end in flux. With the fluxed end facing down towards the charcoal block, use the hot part of a flame to heat and melt the end into a ball. As the end of the wire forms a ball, allow it to travel up the wire until it reaches the desired size. Cool and pickle the wire.

8. Cut the wires to length and use snipe-nose pliers to make a bend in the wire immediately below the ball. Form a small loop on the end of a length of wire of the same dimension and solder the loop shut. Pass a balled wire through the loop. This wire then has a loop formed and soldered and another balled wire is inserted into this loop. Continue until the desired length is created.

7.

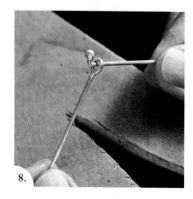

8.

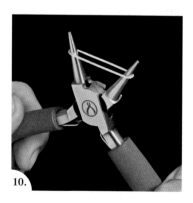

10.

THE PROCESS: SAILOR'S CHAIN

9. Create enough jump rings to make the chain from 18-gauge (1mm) round wire using a 20mm (¾in) mandrel. Close and solder all the rings.

10. Use round-nose pliers to stretch each ring into an elongated oval shape. To ensure uniformity in shape, position every ring in the same place on the pliers each time.

11. Use round-nose pliers to bend the elongated oval in half.

12. Squeeze the loop into shape with pliers and two scribers held at right angles to each other. Secure one scriber in a bench vice and place the larger end of the loop over it. Hold the other scriber by hand with its point inserted through the smaller loop. Use snipe-nose pliers to squeeze the loop both vertically and horizontally at the gap between the two scribers.

13. Push both loops down on a scriber to refine their shape. Squeeze the larger loops together using flat-nose or parallel pliers.

14. Put the chain together by slotting one loop on to another.

15. Squeeze the loops together with pliers to close them. Carry out any necessary cleaning with files and emery paper, followed by pumice powder and a brass brush, then barrel polishing.

12.

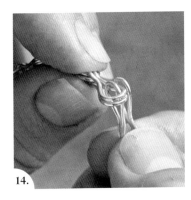

14.

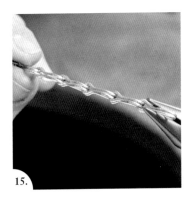

15.

Articulated cuff-link fitting.

Silver earring hook/loop.

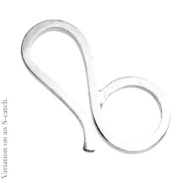

Variation on an S-catch.

FINDINGS AND MECHANISMS

Findings and mechanisms include ear studs and hooks, cuff-link backs, brooch fittings, clasps, catches, pendant fittings/bails and hinges. They perform a vital function by providing a means of attaching a piece of jewellery, or, as in the case of a hinge, providing movement for a particular part, such as a brooch pin.

There are a wide range of manufactured findings to suit just about every requirement. However, a handmade piece of jewellery will, in most cases, benefit from a fitting that has been designed and made specifically for that piece. Not only does this give more scope for solving awkward fitting problems, it also allows the fitting to be designed to complement the piece or be incorporated as a feature.

In most cases sterling silver is used for findings, using half-hard material and work hardening by twisting, burnishing or barreling. Brooch pins are usually more secure when they are made from a harder metal, such as fine stainless-steel wire.

EAR FITTINGS

These include ear posts, scrolls, hooks and loops. Scrolls are usually bought ready-made: ear posts can be bought or made. To make your own post, use 19- or 20-gauge (0.8mm or 0.9mm) wire at a length of 1cm (⅜in). When soldering an ear wire on to a piece, drill a hole for the end of the wire to sit in; if this is not possible, create a larger surface area by soldering a small jump ring to the base of the wire before soldering to the piece. To ensure that the post is strong enough, it should be twisted using pliers and then burnished.

Ear hooks and loops are formed using a combination of mandrels and pliers and need to be work hardened by tapping the curved part with a planishing hammer on a steel block. The ends of ear hooks and loops must be rounded for pushing through the earlobe.

Variation on an S-catch.

Silver box catch showing the tongue sliding into the box.

Heavy brooch with a double stainless steel pin and catches made from rectangular silver wire.

BROOCH FITTINGS

Brooch fittings usually come in parts and comprise a catch, hinge and pin. The pin movement comes from the hinge, which can be achieved by coiling the pin wire to make a spring, then extending it so it becomes the pin stem. Other brooch pin hinges are riveted into place as a final step, creating a small bend or kink in the pin wire near the hinge to provide some springiness to keep the end of the pin in the catch. Catches should be secure enough to hold the end of the pin in place and made so that extra pressure is required to push the pin out to release it. Brooch fittings are usually positioned with the hinge on the right and the catch on the left, facing downwards. The hinge and catch can be placed the opposite way round, but the catch should always be facing downwards as the weight of the brooch will then prevent the pin from coming undone.

CUFF-LINK BACKS

These can be rigid or articulated by the use of a bar, chain or a swivel fitting. A cuff link with a rigid fitting usually has one larger end and one smaller end, with a bar attached to both parts: the smaller end pushes through the cuff. A fitting created from chain is attached to the back of each piece with a loop made from half a jump ring. A swivel back pivots so that one end can be aligned with the central bar and easily inserted through the cuff. Once through, the swivel is pivoted back to secure the cuff link.

PENDANT FITTINGS/BAILS

Bails are the parts that provide a place for forms to be hung from by chain, cord, etc., to create a pendant. Tube or jump rings are often used for this type of fitting. This part is normally the last to be soldered on.

CLASPS AND CATCHES

These are used to join opposite ends of bracelets, necklaces and pendants. Simple S-shaped catches can be made from sterling silver wire; these are suitable for many fastening situations. This type of catch must be work hardened by planishing or barrel polishing. A toggle catch is another simple fastening solution – a bar passes through a ring and when it is worn, the weight of the piece prevents the catch from coming undone. A box catch provides a secure fitting. It consists of a box that holds a catch (a sprung piece of metal called a tongue), which slides into an opening in the box and clicks shut behind a wall. Depressing the tongue and sliding it out from the box releases it. These catches rely on precision: the spring of the tongue and the fit as it slides into the box are crucial to their success. It should slide smoothly and make a pleasing click as the tongue locates and springs up behind the wall.

HINGES

Hinges are made from tube that is accurately cut using a tube cutter and referred to as knuckles: there are usually an odd number of knuckles, all at the same length. Standard tube is suitable to use, but for hinges that will receive a large amount of wear and tear, use joint tube, which has a thicker wall. The knuckles are soldered into a groove or channel alternately to each piece and then joined using a length of wire that is the same size as the inside of the tube. The wire is riveted at the ends.

FINDINGS AND MECHANISMS TUTORIAL
Ear Hooks

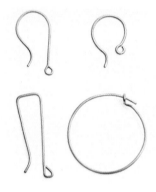

YOU WILL NEED

- 18- and 19-gauge (1.0mm and 0.9mm) round sterling silver wire
- Round-nose, flat-nose, snipe-nose and half-round pliers
- Wire cutters
- 1 and 2cm (⅜ and ¾in) mandrels
- Planishing hammer
- Steel block
- Barrette-needle file, cut 2

THE PROCESS

1. Wrap a length of 18-gauge (1.0mm) round silver wire twice around a 2cm (¾in) diameter mandrel forming a coil.

2. Remove the coil from the mandrel and use round-nose pliers to form a small loop on one end.

3. Use flat-nose pliers to turn the loop 90°.

4. Use round-nose pliers to make a small kink just below the loop to lower it. Cut the wire so that there is a sufficient amount to pass through the loop when the ear hook is closed. File and sand the cut end of the wire to create a rounded, smooth and comfortable end.

5. Planish the ear hook on a steel block to harden it.

6. Use round-nose pliers to make a closed loop at one end of a 6cm (2⁹⁄₁₆in) length of 19-gauge (0.9mm) round silver wire. File and sand the opposite end to create a rounded, smooth, and comfortable end.

7. Form the wire around a 1cm (⅜in) diameter mandrel.

8. Use half-round pliers to curve the end of the hook and refine the shape of the ear loop.

9. Place the ear loop on a steel block and work harden the curved section with a planishing hammer.

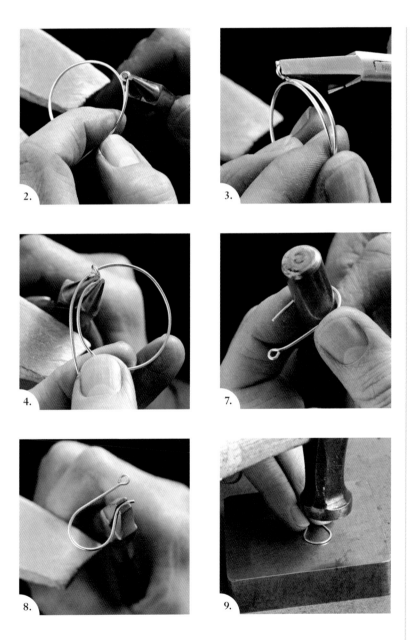

2.

3.

4.

7.

8.

9.

Always work harden the wire after forming to strengthen the ear hook by planishing it on a steel block.

To ensure you make a matching pair of ear loops, carry out each step on both wires at the same time, instead of finishing one loop completely and then starting work on the other.

Make sure loops and hooks are long enough so that they do not fall out of the ear. Check the weight of any part that will be hung from the loop.

Ends must be rounded and comfortable for pushing through the earlobe.

Doming punches make good mandrels.

FINDINGS AND MECHANISMS TUTORIAL

Simple Brooch Fitting and Catch for a Double or Single Pin

YOU WILL NEED

- 12-gauge (2.0mm O/D) sterling silver tube
- 18-gauge (1.0mm) round sterling silver wire
- Small silver jump ring
- 20-gauge (0.8mm) round stainless steel wire
- Rectangular sterling silver wire
- Tube cutter and piercing saw
- Hand file, cut 2
- Barrette-needle file, cut 2
- Emery paper
- Flat-nose, snipe-nose and parallel pliers
- Torch
- Tweezers
- Soldering probe
- Fire brick
- Hard and medium silver solder
- Flux and pickle
- Centre punch
- Jobbing hammer
- Drill bit
- Bench drill or pendant drill

THE PROCESS: SIMPLE BROOCH FITTING

1. Using a tube cutter and piercing saw, cut a short length of 12-gauge (2.0mm) tube. Holding the tube end-to-end in parallel pliers, file a small flat area along the length of the tube.

2. Clean, degrease and flux the reverse side of the brooch. Place the tube flat side down and place small pieces of hard solder in position. Solder the tube to the brooch.

3. To form the catch, cut a length of 18-gauge (1.0mm) round silver wire and file one end flat. To give a larger surface area to attach the wire to the brooch, solder a very small jump ring to the filed end using hard silver solder. Check and mark the position for the catch on the reverse of the brooch, then solder the jump ring and wire in place using medium silver solder.

4. After pickling, use parallel pliers to twist the length of wire to harden it.

5. Cut the wire, leaving it long enough to form into a catch, and file the end. Use round-nose pliers to curl it down and create the catch.

2.

4.

6. Use flat-nose pliers to make a 90° bend in a length of 20-gauge (0.8mm) round stainless-steel wire. Place the short end through the tube, then, using the flat-nose pliers, bend it twice to form a triangle and bend the end of the wire down towards the back of the brooch causing the pin to lift up. Cut the pin to length so that there is enough wire to hold the pin securely in the catch. File the end of the pin to a point using a hand file, then sand it smooth.

THE PROCESS: CATCH FOR A DOUBLE OR SINGLE PIN

7. For a double pin, prepare both pieces alongside each other. Drill a small hole slightly off centre and a short way in from one end of a rectangular piece of silver wire.

8. Rest the wire against a bench peg, while using a piercing saw to make two cuts from the end of the wire up to the hole. Make the first cut on the diagonal, starting just up from the bottom edge, and make the second from the centre.

9. Use a barrette-needle file to refine the shape of the cuts carefully.

10. Cut and file the rectangular wire into a square then paper it in preparation for soldering to the back of the brooch with medium silver solder.

HINTS & TIPS

Give careful consideration to the positioning of the brooch pin. It is usually placed above the centre of the brooch to prevent it from tipping when it's worn.

Sterling silver is usually too weak to make brooch pins. It can be used for lightweight pieces and must be twisted to work harden it. Thin stainless-steel dental wire can be used to make a good, strong pin.

The opening of the catch should be facing downwards when the brooch is worn, because the weight of the brooch prevents the pin from coming undone.

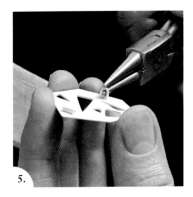

5.

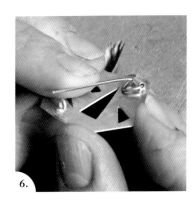

6.

8.

FINDINGS AND MECHANISMS TUTORIAL
Cuff-Link Fitting, Rigid Fitting and Pendant Fitting

YOU WILL NEED
- Piercing saw and blades
- Hand file, cut 2
- Emery paper
- Flat-nose pliers
- Steel block
- Torch
- Soldering bricks
- Tweezers
- Soldering probe
- Flux
- Hard silver solder
- Pickle

FOR CUFF-LINK FITTINGS
- Silver cuff links
- 21-gauge (0.7mm) sterling silver sheet
- 5mm (¹³⁄₆₄in) diameter sterling silver jump ring or round wire
- 12-gauge (2.2mm) sterling-silver wire/rod
- Centre punch
- Jobbing hammer
- Size 54 and 60 drill bit (1.3mm and 0.9mm)
- Bench drill or pendant drill
- Safety glasses
- Reverse-action tweezers

FOR PENDANT FITTINGS
- Silver pendant
- Sterling silver tube
- Tube cutter
- Medium silver solder

THE PROCESS: CUFF-LINK FITTING

1. Cut two pieces of 21-gauge (0.7mm) silver sheet at 4 x 15mm (⁴⁄₁₆ x ¹⁰⁄₁₆in). Round both ends and file the long edges straight and flat.

2. Using the size 54 drill (1.3mm), drill holes in either end of both pieces.

3. Cut a 5mm (¹³⁄₆₄in) jump ring in half to form two loops. Using the size 60 drill (0.9mm), drill two holes in the back of each cuff-link part for the ends of the loop to secure into.

4. With one of the pieces of prepared sheet from Steps 1 and 2 held in reverse-action tweezers, hook a loop through the lower hole in the sheet and secure the ends in the two holes in the back of the cuff link. Solder the loop into position using hard silver solder.

5. After pickling, repeat Step 4 on the smaller shape.

THE PROCESS: RIGID FITTING

6. Create a rigid cuff-link fitting from two 11mm (⁷⁄₁₆in) straight lengths of 12-gauge (2.2mm) round silver wire/rod. File the ends of the rod straight: then, holding the rod in reverse-action tweezers, run medium silver solder on to one end. Position this end centrally on the back of the larger cuff link and rerun the solder to join the two.

4.

6.

THE PROCESS: PENDANT FITTING

7. Cut a small length of silver tube using a piercing saw and a tube cutter.

8. Chamfer the tube using a hand file. File a flat area on the bottom of the tube to increase the surface area for soldering.

9. Mark the position of the fitting on the pendant and position the piece between two soldering bricks to prevent it from moving. Place the tube in position with its flat area down, then flux and solder it using medium silver solder.

10. After pickling, file and clean the piece using emery paper.

HINTS & TIPS

Consider the form, weight and size of the cuff link when deciding on a fitting.

Cuff-link fittings should be secure, as well as easy for the wearer to use.

When soldering a very small component to a much larger part, extra care is needed to make sure that the small component does not get too hot. Direct heat should be kept away from small parts; instead, the heat should be concentrated on the larger piece. This in turn will heat anything smaller that is in direct contact with it.

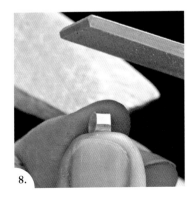

8.

9.

10.

FINDINGS AND MECHANISMS TUTORIAL
S-Clasp, Elongated S-Clasp and Toggle Clasp

YOU WILL NEED

- 12-, 15-, and 17-gauge (2mm, 1.5mm, 1.2mm) round sterling silver wires and 15-gauge (1.5mm) square sterling silver wire
- 18-, 14-, and 10-gauge (1mm, 1.65mm and 2.5mm) round sterling silver wire
- 4mm (⁴⁄₁₆in), 7mm (⁵⁄₁₆in), and 1cm (³⁄₈in) diameter mandrels
- Flat-nose, snipe-nose, round-nose and parallel pliers
- Piercing saw and blades
- Wire cutters
- Needle file
- Emery paper
- Torch
- Tweezers
- Fire brick
- Flux
- Hard and medium silver solder
- Pickle

THE PROCESS: S-CLASP

1. Coil a length of 15-gauge (2mm) round silver wire four times around a 7mm (⁵⁄₁₆in) mandrel. Remove the coil and cut it from the length of wire.

2. Using a pair of flat-nose pliers, lift the first loop away from the main part of the coil.

3. Cut the next loop, leaving the two rings joined.

4. Flatten the two loops using pliers and then neaten both ends using a file and emery paper. Finally, planish the catch on a steel block using a planishing hammer to work harden it.

3.

4.

THE PROCESS: ELONGATED S-CLASP

5.　Melt a ball on to both ends of a length of 17-gauge (1.2mm) round silver wire. After pickling, form the wire into an elegant S-shaped clasp using half-round and round-nose pliers. Work harden the clasp by planishing the curved parts on a steel block using a planishing hammer.

THE PROCESS: TOGGLE CLASP

6.　Make one jump ring from 14-gauge (1.65mm) round silver wire using a 1cm (⅜in) diameter mandrel. Make five jump rings from 18-gauge (1.0mm) round silver wire using a 4mm (³⁄₁₆in) diameter mandrel and cut one of these in half.

7.　Cut a 21mm (¾in) length of 10-gauge (2.5mm) round silver wire to form the bar of the toggle clasp.

8.　Solder shut the largest jump ring and two of the smaller jump rings using hard silver solder.

9.　Solder the loop that was formed from cutting a small jump ring in half (Step 5) to the middle of the 10-gauge (2.5mm) length of wire using hard silver solder. After pickling, file the ends of the wire to an angle using a flat-hand file, then finish with emery paper.

10.　Use the two remaining jump rings to join the parts together and solder them shut.

HINTS & TIPS

Use pliers carefully to avoid marking the wire.

Clasps formed from wire should be work hardened by planishing against a steel block.

S-shaped catches can have one end soldered closed, leaving the other end as the part that is used to perform the opening and closing.

A toggle clasp can easily be adapted to suit many designs. But to ensure it does not come undone, the bar should always be made longer than the measurement of the diameter of the ring through which it passes.

The chain on the bar of a toggle clasp must be long enough for the bar to pass through the ring.

5.

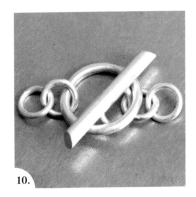

10.

FINDINGS AND MECHANISMS TUTORIAL
Box Catch

YOU WILL NEED

- Sterling silver sheet
- Scriber and dividers
- Square and ruler
- Vernier gauge
- Square needle file
- Tin snips
- Parallel and flat-nose pliers
- Piercing saw and blades
- Flat-hand file, cut 2
- Barrette-needle file, cut 2
- Emery paper
- Steel block
- Planishing hammer
- Torch
- Tweezers
- Soldering probe
- Flux
- Fire brick
- Hard and medium silver solder
- Pickle
- Small drill bit
- Centre punch
- Jobbing hammer
- Pendant motor or bench drill
- Brass brush and pumice powder

THE PROCESS

1. Cut a 70 x 5mm (2¾ x ¹³⁄₆₄in) piece of 20-gauge (0.8mm) silver sheet and file one long and one short edge square and flat. Using a ruler, scriber and a square, mark three lines on the strip, the first 1cm (⅜in) from the straight end, the second ¹⁰⁄₁₆" (1.5cm) from the first line, and the third 1cm (⅜in) from the second line.

2. Use a square file to file a groove along the width of the strip at each marked line, keeping the file perpendicular to the long edge. Use parallel pliers to bend the strip 90° at these points creating an open box form.

3. Secure the box form with binding wire and solder all four corners with hard silver solder. After pickling, cut the excess sheet from one corner and neaten with a file. Paper both edges flat.

4. Solder a 23-gauge (0.6mm) sheet of silver on to one side of the open box using hard silver solder. After pickling, cut the excess sheet and file it back to the walls of the box.

5. Create the opening for the tongue. Use a piercing saw to remove almost all of one of the end walls by cutting a wide U-shape into it. Cut out a shape from the top sheet to form a space for the trigger to sit in. Use a needle file to file up the cut edges, keeping them straight.

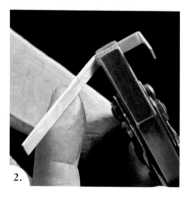

2.

5.

72

6. With the box still open, make the tongue so that it can be easily inserted to check the fit. Cut a strip of 24-gauge (0.5mm) silver sheet slightly wider than the box and twice as long. File the strip along its long edges and refine the tongue opening with a file until the strip slides tightly into the box.

7. To form the trigger, solder a small piece of 3mm (⅛in) square silver wire to one end of the tongue strip, making sure it is positioned centrally and just in from the end.

8. Measure the inside length of the box with a vernier gauge. Deduct a fractionally small amount from this and mark the measurement on the tongue from the trigger end using a scriber and a square to make sure it's perpendicular to the long edge.

9. Fold the tongue over on the scribed line using parallel pliers and close the fold using flat-nose pliers.

(Tutorial continues overleaf.)

HINTS & TIPS

Square corners and parallel sides are crucial to the success of a box catch.

Make the box before the tongue. Use the interior measurements of the box as a guide for the size of the tongue. Cut the material for the tongue slightly wider than needed and file to fit tightly in the box.

For a successful catch the tongue should not be any shorter than 1cm (⅜in).

Silver may not be durable enough for a smaller box catch. Use white gold or stainless steel instead.

Don't use excess solder when soldering the walls of the box together and the top sheet to the box. The inside seams need to be neat and crisp for the tongue to work properly.

Accurate measuring is important for making a successful catch.

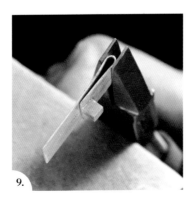

6.
9.

Box Catch Continued

10. Planish the tongue along the fold on a steel block using a planishing hammer.

11. Prise open the tongue with a modelling tool.

12. Test the fit of the tongue in the box and make any adjustments by carefully filing the edges of the tongue.

13. Cut the excess sheet forming the underside of the tongue using a piercing saw, then file it to shape and drill a small hole to attach the catch.

14. To close the box, solder an extra long piece of 23-gauge (0.6mm) silver sheet with medium silver solder to the open side, leaving the extra length of sheet at one end to create a place for linking. After pickling, cut off and file back the excess sheet from the long sides and one narrow end *only*, leaving the extra length of sheet at the other end.

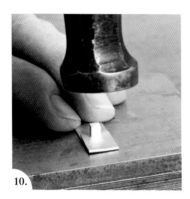

10.

11.

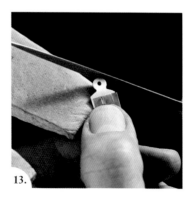

13.

15. Cut the remaining excess sheet using a piercing saw to match the shape created on the tongue in Step 13. File to shape and drill a small hole to attach the catch to the piece.

16. Test the fit of the tongue in the box, checking carefully to see that the top of the tongue springs up behind the end wall as it clicks into place. Depress the trigger to release the tongue from behind the wall and slide it out from the box. Prise the tongue apart a little more to make any necessary adjustments to the fit.

17. Once a satisfactory fit has been achieved, paper and finish the box catch with a brass brush and liquid soap.

HINTS & TIPS

The basic structure – the box – can take any form. Its exterior can easily be altered to blend in or pick up detail from the rest of the piece.

It is very important that the tongue slides tightly into the box without any side to side movement.

The dimensions can be altered to suit.

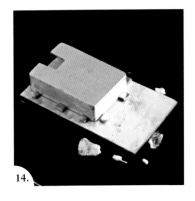

14.

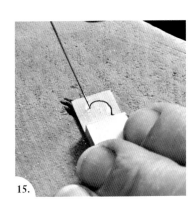

15.

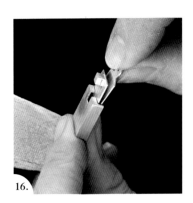

16.

FINDINGS AND MECHANISMS TUTORIAL
Hinges

YOU WILL NEED

- Sterling silver joint tube
- Straight piece of sterling silver wire to fit exactly inside joint tube
- Steel rod to fit exactly inside joint tube
- Tube cutter
- Piercing saw and blades
- Hand file, cut 2
- Emery paper
- Round-needle file
- Barrette-needle file, cut 2
- Torch
- Tweezers
- Soldering probe and brick
- Flux
- Hard silver solder
- Ball or bud burr
- Pendant motor
- Wire cutters
- Snipe-nose pliers
- Steel block
- Ball-peen hammer

THE PROCESS

1. Cut three knuckles using a tube cutter and piercing saw. All three need to be the same length.

2. With a cut 2 hand file resting on the bench peg, file the ends of each knuckle flat by carefully dragging the tube forwards along the file, turning it a little after each stroke.

3. Using a round needle file, create a channel for the knuckles to sit in along both edges of the parts to be joined.

4. Slot the knuckles on to the steel rod.

5. Place both parts being joined with the hinge on a soldering brick with a sheet of metal underneath each one to raise them up a little so that they are at the correct height for the knuckles. Position the knuckles, still on the steel rod, in-between the parts, flux the piece at the three joining points taking care not to use excess flux. Place small pieces of hard silver solder in position.

6. Heat and tack solder the piece. Remove the steel rod and carefully separate the two pieces so that the knuckles can be safely soldered without the danger of the solder running and joining a knuckle to the wrong part. After pickling, reinsert the steel rod so that the soldering and hinge movement can be checked. Use a barrette-needle file to clean up the solder where necessary and use emery paper to finish.

7. Countersink both ends of the tube by widening the opening of the holes with a bud or ball burr in a pendant motor.

8. Secure the straight silver wire in the protective jaws of a bench vice. File the end flat, then tap it with a ball-peen hammer to spread the metal and create a rivet head.

9. Put the two halves of the hinge together using the piece of straight silver wire with the formed rivet head.

10. Cut the wire, leaving a small end protruding. File this end flat. Working on a flat steel block, tap the end of the wire with a ball-peen hammer to spread the metal into the countersunk hole forming the rivet head and completing the hinge.

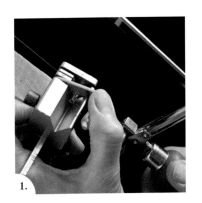

1.

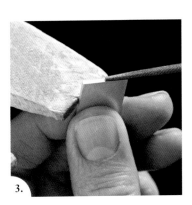

3.

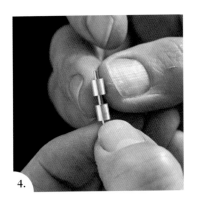

4.

5.

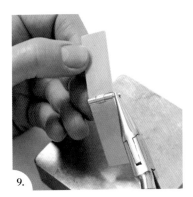

9.

10.

HINTS & TIPS

Standard tube can be used for hinges, but for pieces that will receive a lot of wear and tear use joint tube because it has a thicker wall.

A successful hinge relies on accurate making and extra care when soldering.

There is usually an odd number of knuckles on a hinge, all the same length.

To ensure the ends of the knuckles are parallel, hold them in a tube block while filing with a flat-hand file.

Use a steel rod the same diameter as the internal hole of the tube to slide the knuckles on and keep them aligned while they are tack soldered in position. The rod can then be removed, the two parts separated, and the knuckles soldered properly without the danger of the solder running and joining a knuckle to the wrong part.

Out of Chaos ring by Birgit Holdinghausen. Photo: Lindsay Cox.

Zopf earrings by Verena Schreppel.

Ring by Nora Rochel. Photo: Nora Rochel.

CASTING

Casting gives form to molten metal through a variety of different processes ranging from simple ancient methods to refined commercial techniques. Sand and cuttlefish casting are one-use moulds that offer low tech, quick and fairly accurate methods. Both of these casting techniques work on a process whereby the molten metal fills the mould through the force of gravity.

Various simple three-dimensional objects can be used as models to make an impression in the cuttlefish or sand, such as shells; stones; buttons; carved wax models; or objects made from plastic, wood or metal. An object with a surface texture works particularly well. In addition to using a model, the cuttlefish can be easily carved to produce a form to cast from.

Clean, solder-free silver scrap can be used for cuttlefish and sand casting, making this an economical use of leftover metal. Estimate the weight of the silver required, but always add on extra for the sprue. Using too much silver can be dangerous as the molten metal can spill over from the pouring channel, however, if you use too little silver, the casting may be incomplete. As a general guide to help estimate the amount, silver is 10 to 11 times the weight of wax.

Casting should be carried out in a well-ventilated room with a safe and sturdy casting area set up using fire bricks; the bricks should cover a large enough area in case there is any overspill of the molten silver.

Because the metal shrinks on cooling, the finished casting will be a little smaller than the original model. Completed silver castings can be quenched and should be pickled to remove oxides. Any texture that has been removed when the sprue was cut off can be recreated using burrs and a pendant drill.

CUTTLEFISH CASTING

Cuttlefish are available from jewellery suppliers, pet stores and can also be found on the beach! The cuttlefish skeleton is lightweight, soft and fragile, but can withstand the heat involved with casting. Large cuttlefish that are fatter around the middle section work better than small, thin ones.

The cuttlefish is prepared by cutting it in half along its length and then sanding the soft side of each half completely flat. For a larger mould, use two cuttlefish instead of one and cut off their pointed ends. Gently pressing a model halfway into the flat face of the cuttlefish will make an impression. Before gently pressing the two halves together, press ball bearings or matchsticks halfway into the cuttlefish, creating locaters to ensure that the two pieces align correctly. Once the pouring funnel has been cut, the two halves are separated and the model removed, leaving the locaters in place. Shallow lines should be carefully cut in one side of the mould to allow air to escape when the molten silver is poured in. The two halves are then placed back together and secured with binding wire in readiness for casting.

The cuttlefish lends itself well to carving and a mould cavity can be created using carving tools. The design should take into account that the molten metal will flow downwards from the pouring funnel and will not flow backwards. Brushing the cuttlefish with a soft paintbrush deepens, and emphasises its natural ridged pattern, giving an interesting surface texture. This technique can be used in combination with impressing a model into the surface or carving a mould cavity away.

SAND CASTING

This technique uses a moist and firmly packed casting sand, which is available from jewellery suppliers. The sand is particularly good at picking up fine surface detail making it possible to produce castings with striking results.

To create the mould the sand is compacted into one half of a two-part frame, a model is pressed halfway into the sand and the two frames placed together. More sand is packed into the second frame and then pounded down. The model must be able to withstand the pressure from this pounding. The two frames are then taken apart and the model carefully removed. A sprue is created through one half of the mould and air vents can be made to allow the air to escape when the molten metal is poured in. However, for small-scale items, the porosity of the sand is usually sufficient to allow the air to escape. A wide pouring funnel is cut to create a passage to enable the molten metal to flow

easily into the mould. The frames are placed back together and the molten metal poured into the mould via the funnel. For a flat-backed casting, the model can be pressed down fully into the sand instead of halfway.

COMMERCIAL CASTING

There are various commercial casting methods available for silver, including the lost wax process. Models for this method can be created from modelling wax using specialist wax files, saw blades and tools to create complex forms. The wax model is destroyed during the casting process, so this is a one-use model. To produce multiple replicas, a vulcanised rubber mould is made of the master. From this mould, waxes are produced and casting is carried out using the lost wax process. Creating a vulcanised rubber mould requires a master made from metal, which can withstand the heat and pressure involved in this particular mould-making process, leaving the master intact.

Freeform rings by Kelvin J. Birk. Photo: Kelvin J. Birk.

CASTING TUTORIAL

Cuttlefish Casting *by Michael Milloy*

YOU WILL NEED

- Cuttlefish
- Carving tools: cocktail stick, wax carving tools, scalpel, punches, scriber
- Piercing saw and blade
- Rough sand paper
- Ball bearings or matchsticks
- Soft paintbrush
- Wire cutters
- Flat-nose pliers
- Binding wire
- Fire bricks
- Crucible/scorifier
- Crucible tongs
- Silver (clean scraps or casting grain)
- Torch with large burner
- Insulated gloves
- Pickling solution
- Pumice powder and brass brush
- Mask
- Pendant motor and burrs
- File
- Emery paper

THE PROCESS

1. Cut a cuttlefish in half using a piercing saw. Rub down the softer side of each half on rough sand paper until it is completely flat so that, when both flat faces are put together, there are no gaps.

2. Carve a pattern in one half, approximately 2cm (1in) from the top, using wax carving tools, a scriber and a scalpel. Brush away the surface of the carved area to emphasise the natural ridges and contours of the cuttlefish.

3. Using a scalpel, make a V-shaped pouring channel from the top edge down to the carved area and make three air vents by creating fine lines in the surface away from the outer edge of the carving.

4. Push three ball bearings halfway into the surface around the carved pattern, creating locaters to ensure the two halves align properly.

5. Gently press the two halves together until their surfaces meet. Holding both together, carve out the second pouring channel.

6. Cut grooves at four locations in the edges so that the two halves can be secured with binding wire. Twist the wire and make small bends along its length around the cuttlefish to tighten and secure it.

7. Create a safe casting area using fire bricks; support the cuttlefish between two bricks. Place small pieces of silver/casting grain in the scorifier and sprinkle with a pinch of Borax powder. Estimate the amount of silver required, adding some extra for the sprue.

8. Using a torch with a large burner, heat the silver to melting point. Once the molten silver is spinning in a ball, carefully lift the scorifier using tongs, and, with the flame directed on the silver to keep it molten, pour the silver into the cuttlefish mould via the pouring channel.

9. After allowing it to cool, take the cuttlefish apart and remove the silver cast. Quench the cast in water, then pickle and clean it with pumice powder and a brass brush. Remove the sprue with a piercing saw, then file and clean the cast with a pendant drill attachment.

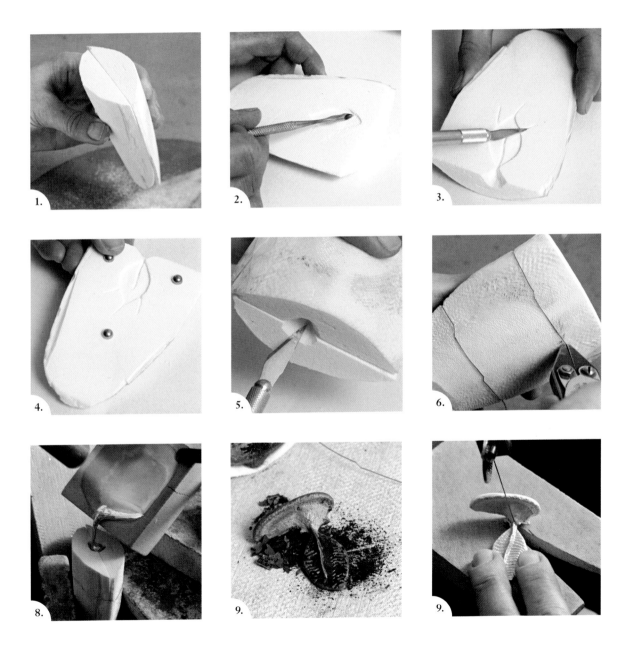

1.

2.

3.

4.

5.

6.

8.

9.

9.

CASTING TUTORIAL

Sand Casting by *Michael Milloy*

YOU WILL NEED

- Suitable object to use as a model
- Casting sand/clay (Delft Clay)
- Aluminium rings/frame
- Steel ruler
- Talcum powder
- Scalpel
- Soft paintbrush
- Drill bit
- Mallet or flat-faced hammer
- Fire bricks
- Crucible/scorifier
- Tongs
- Silver (clean scrap or casting grain)
- Torch with large burner
- Insulated gloves
- Pickling solution
- Files
- Pendant motor and burrs
- Emery paper
- Pumice powder and brass brush

THE PROCESS

1. Pack the narrower aluminium ring with the lip with casting sand. Pound the sand down with a flat-faced hammer to compress it. Add extra sand and level the top of the sand with a steel ruler.

2. Press your chosen object halfway down into the clay. To ensure the mould will come apart at the next stage without the sand sticking, dust the surface lightly with talcum powder.

3. Place the second aluminium ring on top of the first, lining up the grooves marked on the outside of each ring. Fill this with the sand, compacting it down, and level it.

4. Take the rings carefully apart and remove your object with a scalpel, taking care not to disturb the sand around it.

5. Use a 3mm (⅛in) drill bit to make the sprue hole. Starting from inside the impression, carefully create the hole in the centre and right the way through the sand. Tip off the excess sand created by this process.

6. Enlarge the top opening of the sprue hole using a scalpel to create a funnel for receiving the molten silver.

7. Reassemble the two halves of the mould, lining up the grooves marked on the outside. Create a safe casting area with fire bricks and position the mould and crucible so that they are not too far apart.

8. Estimate the amount of silver required, adding some extra for the sprue. Place this in the scorifier and sprinkle with Borax powder. Use a torch with a large burner to heat the silver to melting point.

9. Once the silver is spinning in a ball, carefully lift the scorifier using tongs and, with the flame directed on to the silver to keep it molten, pour the silver into the mould via the pouring channel.

10. Allow the mould to cool in situ before placing it on a steel block to fully cool. Open the mould and remove the casting from the sand. Pickle it, then clean it with pumice powder and a brass brush.

11. Remove the sprue with a piercing saw and file away the remainder, use a burr in a pendant drill to redefine the surface of this area. Give a final finish with emery paper, then a brass brush and liquid soap.

1.

2.

3.

4.

5.

6.

8.

9.

10.

Cuff by Darren Harvey. Photo: Darren Harvey.

Kingfisher brooch by Hannah Louise Lamb.
Photo: Hannah Louise Lamb.

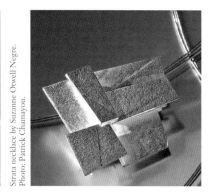

Strata necklace by Suzanne Otwell Negre.
Photo: Patrick Chamayou.

TEXTURING

Silver is soft, malleable and easily receives pattern and texture from rolling mills, hammers or punches. Before texturing, the silver must be annealed to make it soft, which will help it to take up the texture more readily (this is particularly important for fine details), and it will also prevent the metal from splitting.

Careful planning is required before you begin to make a textured piece. The stage at which the piece will be textured may be dictated by the process used, for example roller printing can only be carried out on flat sheet, so all fabrication and forming needs to take place after texturing. Hammer texturing a ring will stretch it to become one or two sizes larger, which needs to be taken into account when deciding which size to make the ring. Further forming of a textured piece should be carried out with care to prevent tools causing damage to the surface; working with wooden formers and placing masking tape over textures will help with this. The texturing process work hardens the silver, so it is important to anneal it prior to further forming.

The finishing of a textured piece also requires careful consideration. Using two different finishing methods on one texture will give a more defined pattern, for example, polishing a textured piece and then giving it a fine emery paper finish across the surface, making sure that the paper does not reach into the recessed areas, will give a satin surface contrasting with polished recesses. Colouring a textured piece of silver defines the pattern and enhances its overall effect. The recesses produced by texturing are ideal areas for the colour to sit in, making it less vulnerable to wear and tear.

HAMMER TEXTURES

Hammer texturing can be used on flat sheet and on some formed pieces. It can be employed in a controlled manner to add detail by texturing targeted areas, or as an overall effect. Minimal hammering can produce a random and subtle result, while working intensively over a surface to build up a particular effect will create a heavily textured piece.

Any hammer will make a mark on silver, but the type of mark depends upon the shape of the hammer head, combined with the force behind the hammer blow. Specialist texturing hammers can be purchased from jewellery tool suppliers. Alternatively, experiment with existing hammers or modify old hammers using files and/or burrs.

Always hammer against a hard surface, such as a steel block or anvil. Formed pieces should be hammered against an appropriate hard steel former such as a mandrel, doming punch or stake. There should be no gaps between the silver and the hard surface. The hammer should always strike the metal so that its head makes full contact with it; if only the edge of the hammer is striking the metal, the desired texture may not be achieved. A flat-faced hammer can be used to hammer another textured material such as fabric or wire against a silver sheet or to hammer the silver against another textured surface, like a piece of concrete. This will imprint a texture into the silver with similar results to roller printing. It is always advisable to experiment on some scrap silver to perfect your hammering technique and to ascertain which hammer will produce what texture before working on the final piece.

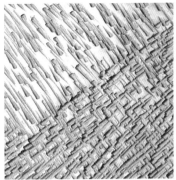

Texture from the narrow end of a pin hammer, on one half the hammer has been worked in two different directions.

Texture created using the round end of a jobbing hammer. The top section was hammered heavily and the bottom section hammered randomly.

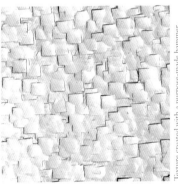

Texture created with a purpose-made hammer.

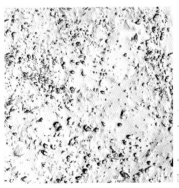

Silver hammered against concrete.

Leaves necklace by Suzanne Orwell Negre. Photo: Photo: Patrick Chamayou.

ROLLER PRINTING

A rolling mill is usually used to reduce the thickness of sheet metal, however, passing a sheet of silver through a rolling mill along with another textured material will emboss the silver with the reverse image of the pattern. This is a quick and easy technique that can produce some stunning results, ranging from subtle to bold.

A vast range of materials are suitable for roller printing, such as watercolour paper, skeleton leaves, feathers, fabric, lace, wire, patterned brass sheet, metal mesh, string, sandpaper, masking tape, net, etc. This gives plenty of scope for experimentation. It's possible to roll two texturing materials together, but if one material is thicker it is likely to dominate any finer material passing through at the same time.

Prepare the silver by annealing, pickling and rinsing it three times, making it very soft with a fine surface. The silver must be dry before it's passed through the rollers. If the rollers become wet, they can rust and their surfaces may be damaged.

Ideally, two sheets of silver should be rolled together with the texturing material placed between them to create a sandwich. This will result in two pieces of textured silver with a mirror image, which is ideal for creating a pair of symmetrical earrings where the pattern needs to be in reverse. In some instances it may not be viable to imprint two pieces of silver at once due to requirements or cost, in which case the metal should be rolled with the texture exposed to the top roller. If the texture material is likely to damage the rollers, then two pieces of silver must be used. Fine texture

materials, like feathers, should be passed through with just a single piece of silver, as the imprint results will be much clearer. Using paper to hold the silver sheet and texture together can help. Be aware that even a smooth paper will leave some sort of subtle imprint on the silver.

Repositioning the texture material after imprinting is impossible. To achieve a good imprint on the silver in one pass, the correct distance must be set between the two rollers so that enough pressure is applied. As a guide, the handle of the rolling mill should be hard to turn but not so difficult that excessive force is required to make just a small move. Set the rollers by eye at first, then test the tension by starting to slowly feed the sandwich through while turning the handle until the rollers bite, then adjust them accordingly.

Cutting and forming usually takes place after the silver has been roller printed, so you will need to texture a larger piece of silver than is actually required. Masking tape can be used to protect the imprinted surface from marks from the cutting and forming tools. Soldering textured silver is not ideal as the solder can run into the recesses of the imprint.

Silver roller printed with a section from a sheet of brass scale models.

Silver roller printed with hole-punched watercolour paper.

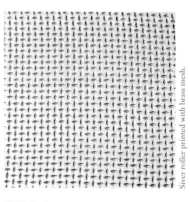

Siver roller printed with brass mesh.

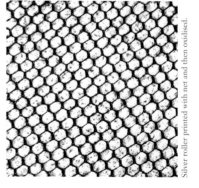

Silver roller printed with net and then oxidised.

STAMPING

Stamping uses decorative punches made from hardened and tempered tool steel, together with a hammer that delivers a blow to the end of the punch, causing it to make an indentation in the silver sheet. Decorative, letter and number punches can be purchased from jewellery suppliers, but you can also make your own bespoke punches from tooling steel. To do this, anneal the steel by heating it to cherry red and allow it to air cool, then use a disc or belt sander to shape the end, followed by files, a piercing saw or burrs to create the design or pattern. To check the pattern, press the end of the punch into something soft, such as clay. The punch must be hardened once it is complete by heating it to a glowing red and immediately quenching it in oil. Polish the punch using wet and dry papers, followed by a polishing mop. The punch should then be tempered to make it less brittle by slowly heating it, starting at the opposite end from the pattern and gradually drawing the heat along the punch until a straw colour appears. The punch should then be quenched in oil.

The thicker the silver sheet, the deeper the impression made by the punch. As a guide, the sheet should be no thinner than 22-gauge (0.6mm) and it should be flat and annealed. Always work on a steel block or former; placing a piece of paper underneath the silver helps to create a deeper impression with the punch. To stamp formed pieces, use an appropriately-shaped steel former to support the work, such as a mandrel or doming punch. The stamping punch must be held at 90° to the silver sheet with its face making full contact with the metal, otherwise the mark it makes will be incomplete and repositioning it can be difficult. Use a jobbing hammer or a repoussé hammer for smaller punches. The mark should be made with a single, sharp hammer blow. Stamping a flat piece of metal will usually cause it to curl, so it will need to be flattened with a mallet against a steel block.

Experimenting on scrap silver is recommended and will help you perfect your technique. Repeated use of the same punch and combinations of different punches can be used to build up patterns and designs.

Three different punches were used to create this pattern.

Oval necklace by Jane Adam. Photo: Joel Degen.

TEXTURING TUTORIAL
Hammer Texturing

YOU WILL NEED

- Selection of hammers
- Silver (sheet, dome and ring)
- Mallet
- Steel binding wire
- Paper
- Steel block/anvil, mandrel and doming punch
- Bench vice
- Parallel pliers
- Torch
- Heat-resistant block
- Steel tweezers
- Pickling solution

THE PROCESS

1. To prepare for hammer texturing, anneal, cool and pickle a piece of silver sheet, then rinse and dry it well.

2. After placing the sheet on a flat steel block, use the rounded end of a repoussé hammer to texture half the silver sheet. Gradually build up a heavy texture.

3. To remove the curl in the sheet created by the hammering process, lay the sheet textured side down on a piece of paper on a steel block and then tap it flat using a mallet.

4. Texture the second section of the silver sheet in the same way using a purpose-made texturing hammer.

5. Wrap steel binding wire around a piece of silver sheet and create angles along the lengths using pliers. Lay the sheet in-between paper and then place it on a steel block.

6. Use a jobbing hammer to hit the silver and steel wire piece while keeping it in between the paper.

7. Texture a silver dome using a doming punch secured in a bench vice as a former. Use the narrow elongated end of a pin hammer to texture the dome.

8. Texture a flat silver band ring using a steel mandrel as a former. Use the narrow elongated end of a pin hammer to texture the ring. After working around the ring once, take it off the mandrel and turn it to avoid the ring becoming narrower on one side and wider on another. Repeat this process until the desired texture is achieved.

9. Place the ring on a steel block and texture around its flat edges using the pin hammer. Slowly turn the ring as the hammer taps.

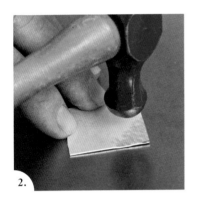

2.

4.

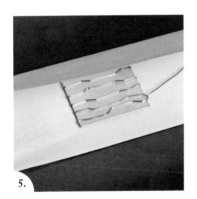

5.

7.

8.

9.

HINTS & TIPS

Always work on a steel block or former and make sure there are no gaps between the two, otherwise the sheet may distort and mis-shape.

Remember that hammering will work harden the silver, so anneal when necessary during the texturing process and always anneal before any further forming.

Texturing rings will cause them to stretch as much as one or two sizes. Take this into account when deciding which size to make the ring.

Flat-band rings and bracelets that are made from sheet can be hammer textured before being formed. Anneal and texture the silver sheet, then anneal it again and form it into a ring or bangle with a solder join. File and paper the join area as necessary, then place the piece on a mandrel and, using the original texture hammer, re-texture the join area to blend it in with the existing texture.

TEXTURING TUTORIAL
Roller Printing

YOU WILL NEED

- Selection of materials
- Rolling mill
- Silver sheet
- Mallet
- Paper
- Steel block
- Torch
- Heat-resistant block
- Steel tweezers
- Pickling solution

THE PROCESS

1. Anneal, cool and pickle two pieces of silver sheet three times to ensure they are soft and have a fine white silver surface. Cut a piece of lace to size and place it between the silver sheets.

2. Set the rolling mill by eye, then adjust it until the sandwich of silver and lace is able to pass through the rollers under pressure.

3. Texture the silver in one single pass.

4. To remove the curl caused by passing the sheet through the rollers, lay the piece between two sheets of paper to protect the texture, and then flatten it on a steel block with a mallet. Clean the imprinted silver with a brass brush and pumice powder and then colour it using liver of sulphur.

1.

2.

3.

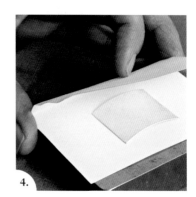

4.

Steps 5–10: Follow the same preparation and roller printing techniques as in Steps 1–4.

5. Apply ripped strips of masking tape to the surface of the silver before passing it through the rolling mill.

6. Randomly curl and place fine copper wire on a silver sheet. Place this between a piece of folded paper and pass it through the rolling mill.

7. Pass a skeleton leaf through the rolling mill with a single sheet of silver, folded between a piece of paper.

8. Attach circular stickers to a sheet of silver, then pass it through the rolling mill. The stickers become elongated, resulting in an oval imprint.

9. Create a subtle imprint by placing a feather on a piece of silver sheet and passing it through the rolling mill between a piece of folded tracing paper.

10. Pass a piece of fabric through the rolling mill with the fabric exposed to the top roller. The imprinted silver is then oxidised with liver of sulphur. Use emery paper to remove the colour from the surface of the silver, leaving colour in the recesses created by the texturing process.

5.

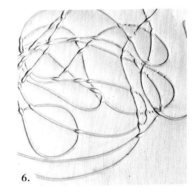

6.

7.

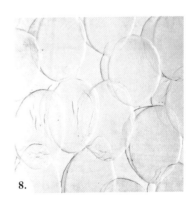

8.

9.

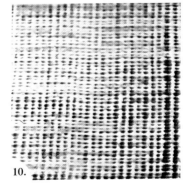

10.

TEXTURING TUTORIAL

Stamping by Michael Milloy

YOU WILL NEED

- Selection of decorative, letter and number punches
- Jobbing and repoussé hammers
- Silver sheet
- Mallet
- Paper
- Steel block
- Torch
- Heat-resistant block
- Steel tweezers
- Pickling solution
- Doming punch
- Centre punch

THE PROCESS

1. Anneal and clean a piece of silver sheet with pumice powder and a brass brush. Place the silver on a sheet of paper on a steel block. Position a punch and hold it at 90° to the silver sheet with its face making full contact with the metal. Use a jobbing hammer to make a single, sharp blow to the end of the punch.

Steps 2–9: Follow the same preparation and stamping techniques as in Step 1.

2. Use four different punches to create this flower and leaf pattern. Polish the silver afterwards.

3. Draw a design on to the silver sheet with a scriber and use a shadowing punch with a repoussé hammer to create the textured area, working up to the scribed line and leaving an area of smooth metal inside it.

4. Use three different punches to create this flower motif.

5. Use a doming punch and a centre punch to create this dimpled pattern.

6. Using a random selection of decorative and letter punches creates an unusual pattern.

7. Use a letter O punch in a random style. To enhance the pattern, oxidise the silver and then remove it from the surface, leaving the colour in the recesses.

8. Use two different punches and a scriber to create this design. Finish the piece with a brass brush, followed by fine emery paper.

9. Use a selection of letter and number punches. Colour some of the recesses by oxidising with Platinol and applying permanent ink with a cocktail stick. Finish the surface with emery paper.

1.

2.

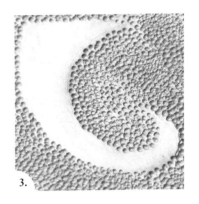

3.

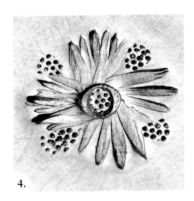

4.

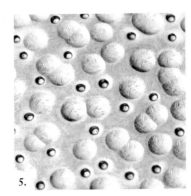

5.

6.

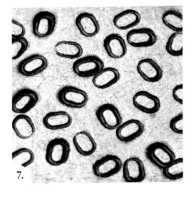

7.

8.

9.

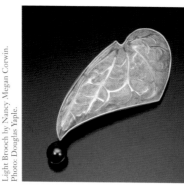

CHASING AND REPOUSSÉ

Chasing – derived from the noun 'chase' meaning furrow, groove or channel – is an intaglio technique used for ornamentation. Repoussé, from the French for pushed, is a shaping technique used to create patterns in relief. Both techniques make use of the plasticity of metal by stretching it using punches and hammers to produce embossed designs. Chasing is carried out on the front of a piece and repoussé from the reverse side; the two techniques are often used in conjunction with each other, when they are jointly referred to as chasing.

Silver is an ideal metal for these techniques because it is particularly malleable; fine and Britannia silver are easier to work than sterling. Chasing and repoussé can be time-consuming techniques because of the various stages that are required and their repetitive nature. However, the process can also be an immensely satisfying one, as you watch the piece slowly form as the silver is manipulated.

Pitch is used to support the metal during chasing and repoussé; its elasticity allows the metal to be pushed out with the punches, while also providing the necessary support. Pitch that is too hard will cause the metal to become thin, but if it's too soft it is difficult to control the form. Ready-made jewellers' pitch can be purchased and typically contains pitch, plaster of Paris and linseed oil or tallow. It is usually placed in a cast iron hemispherical bowl that sits on a wooden ring or sandbag, so that the bowl can easily be tilted and turned when working. The pitch is gently warmed with a torch to make it pliable before setting the metal on it; it's then allowed to cool and become firm before working the metal. The pitch can be used repeatedly providing it is not overheated – heating the pitch until it bubbles and smokes evaporates the oil in it, making it brittle.

The ideal thickness of silver for chasing and repoussé work is 20–22-gauge (0.6–0.8mm). It must be annealed before work commences on it and again during its forming as it becomes work hardened. Remove the piece regularly from the pitch to both anneal and to work the opposing side. The pitch can be removed from the metal with turpentine or burnt away with a torch. Work in a well-ventilated area when burning the pitch.

CHASING

The chasing technique creates lines and details on either a flat or a formed piece of metal using a tracer or liner punch; these have narrow but slightly rounded ends so that they do not cut into the metal. The technique can be used alone to add detail or to trace a design out prior to repoussé work. It is similar to stamping, but instead of the punch being struck once, it is tapped continuously with a chasing or repoussé hammer while holding the punch at a slight angle away from the body; this encourages the punch to move forwards, incising a thin line in the metal.

REPOUSSÉ

For repoussé work, the chased line should be visible on the reverse side. Once the design has been chased on to the silver, the piece is turned over and worked on from the back using smooth modelling and doming punches to push the metal out, creating raised areas on the front. The repoussé technique does not thin the metal, but it can split if it is not annealed once it becomes work hardened.

When the repoussé work is complete, the piece is removed from the pitch and cleaned and annealed. It is then placed back in the pitch so that it can be worked on further from the front using planishing punches to smooth and level the metal, and chasing punches to decorate and define the form. Additional details can be created using matting punches. The hollow shapes created by the repoussé technique can be filled with warm pitch before placing the piece back in the pitch bowl, front side up; this allows the raised areas to be worked on from the front without their forms distorting.

CHASING AND REPOUSSÉ TOOLS

The chasing or repoussé hammer has a large, round, flat face that will easily hit the end of the punch, and a narrow shaft that broadens out to sit in the palm of the hand; it should be used with a rhythmical tapping action. The punches should be approximately 10cm (4in) long and can be purchased or made from hardened tool steel that is ground or filed to shape and polished.

Continuously hammering the punch causes the metal to spread at the top end; to counteract this, the ends of punches should be chamfered. The face of a punch must not be sharp, otherwise it may cut into the silver. A basic set of around 20 punches should include: straight and curved lining or tracing punches for marking out a design and refining; modelling punches for pushing the metal into shape; doming punches for forming rounded and raised areas; large, flat-faced planishing punches for leveling, smoothing and polishing; and matting punches, which have patterns or textures and are used to create texture and also cover marks made by other tools. You will need a large collection of punches because several different sizes of the same punch will be required when working.

Once you have a basic set, you can also make your own punches from tool steel, hardening and tempering them before use. Flat-faced hardwood punches are useful for flattening distorted areas and can be used when the piece is placed on a flat surface, such as a steel block.

CHASING AND REPOUSSÉ TUTORIAL

YOU WILL NEED

- Fine or Britannia silver sheet
- Pitch bowl
- Sandbag or ring
- Chasing and repoussé punches
- Chasing/repoussé hammer
- Parallel pliers
- Small mallet
- Wooden punch or flat-faced piece of hardwood
- Torch
- Fire brick
- Steel tweezers
- Water
- Pickle
- Turpentine
- Paper towel
- Pencil
- Scriber or permanent black marker pen
- Emery paper
- Pumice powder
- Brass brush

THE PROCESS

1. Anneal and clean a piece of fine or Britannia silver sheet. Give it an emery-papered surface before drawing the design on with a pencil. Bend the four corners of the silver over using parallel pliers to help anchor the sheet in the pitch.

2. Warm the pitch gently with a soft flamed torch and place the sheet on the pitch using steel tweezers. Press it down using the end of a doming punch to make sure that the surface is level with the pitch. Use wet fingers to push the warmed soft pitch over at each side.

3. Allow the pitch to cool and become firm before chasing. With the pitch bowl supported on a ring, mark the design using a chasing hammer and chisel-shaped lining punch. Hold the punch between your thumb and index finger, with the third and fourth fingers sitting below these and supporting the punch and the little finger rested against the metal or pitch. Hold the punch at a slight angle away from the body and tap with light, rhythmic blows, forcing the punch forwards, following the marked-out design and creating a thin, continuous line. Use a curved lining punch for the tight curve within the design.

4. Remove the metal from the pitch by gently warming it and prising it out with tweezers. In a well-ventilated area, burn the pitch off the silver and then clean, rinse and dry it.

5. Bend back the four corners of the silver the opposite way using parallel pliers. As in Step 3, warm the pitch and place the silver with its reverse side uppermost. Once the pitch has cooled, form the raised area using several different-sized doming punches and a chasing hammer. Use the same technique as in Step 3, but work the doming punches repeatedly over the surface with their marks overlapping each other as they push the metal out.

6. Once the silver has become work hardened, remove it from the pitch as in Step 5, then anneal and clean it before returning it for further forming. Use smaller modelling punches to form the narrower areas.

7. Once a satisfactory form has been achieved, remove the silver from the pitch and clean it. Place it on a steel block and use a small mallet to flatten the surrounding metal that has become distorted by the repoussé process. Use a flat-faced piece of wood to flatten closer to the raised area.

8. Return the piece to the pitch once again with the front uppermost. Level the areas close to the raised form that could not be reached with the wooden punch with various flat-faced punches and a chasing hammer. Use a lining tool to define the line around the form.

9. Remove the piece from the pitch and clean it. Cut the form from the sheet using a piercing saw. Sand it across the back to level it and finish the front with emery paper, pumice powder and a brass brush. The piece is then ready for any further work, such as soldering a sheet of silver to the back.

HINTS & TIPS

Always work in a well-ventilated area, especially when burning the pitch off the silver. This can be done outside if a suitable fire brick is used.

Start with a larger piece of silver than required to allow for distortion of the surrounding metal.

3.

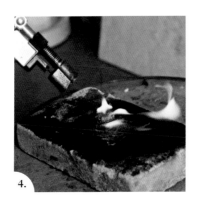

4.

5.

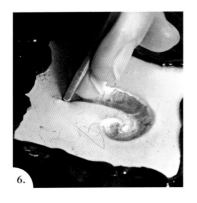

6.

7.

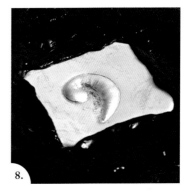

8.

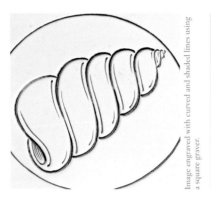

Image engraved with curved and shaded lines using a square graver.

Letter engraved with curved and straight lines using a square graver. The lines were then oxidised.

ENGRAVING

Engraving is the technique of making incisions in the surface of a metal using a hardened steel tool called a graver (also known as a scorper). It is often used to provide recesses for enamelling, and the incised lines can be oxidised to enhance the overall effect. Hand engraving is a highly-skilled technique that requires patience and many hours of practice. Elaborate engraving work is best carried out by a professional who has spent years perfecting their technique.

Silver is softer than other precious metals, making the surface easier to cut into with the graver, but this does not necessarily make the technique any easier. It is possible for a beginner to learn sufficient engraving skills to produce basic straight and curved lines, as well as texturing. Once these basics have been mastered, they can be put together to create simple designs and patterns. Engraving is a good technique to learn in general, as a graver can be used to refine details and clean up areas on a piece.

GRAVERS

Gravers come in a variety of shapes and sizes, with each one producing a different-shaped cutting end. (See illustration opposite.) Gravers are sold in standard lengths without handles so that the correct length can be set for each individual.

To determine the correct length for you, hold the handle and the graver together in the palm of your hand, with your thumb extended along the length of the graver. The cutting end should extend about 1.3–3.4cm (½–1¼in) beyond the end of the thumb; the total length of the graver and handle should be about 9–10cm (3½–4in). Mark off the tang of the graver, allowing extra for securing in the handle. Use a bench vice to hold the graver. Filing or grinding around the mark will allow the excess to be easily snapped off. Insert the tang into the neck of the handle and tap it down with a mallet to make it secure. Once the handle has been secured, the graver should be sharpened (most gravers are sharpened to an angle of 45°), by running the cutting face up and down on an oilstone that has had three-in-one oil applied to it. The face should be kept completely flat against the oilstone and at the same angle throughout the process. Stabbing the end into a piece of hardwood several times will remove any burrs. Both square and lozenge-shaped gravers need to have a small amount of the underside of the cutting face removed to change the angle that the graver cuts at to 5°. The graver is finally polished, repeating the same technique using an Arkansas stone.

ENGRAVING TECHNIQUE

Engraving is often the last process carried out on a piece, so the surface of the silver should be prepared with its final finish. The pattern or design is transferred to the metal by dabbing the surface with plasticine and then applying French chalk. The design can then be drawn out using a plastic or wooden pointed tool, allowing any mistakes to be easily rectified before using a scriber to finally mark the design out.

Engraving is a controlled action and it is important that the work is held securely in an engraver's vice or, for larger and more awkward-shaped pieces, on a sandbag or taped to a block of wood. The work should be carried out at chest height and may need to be done at a table, rather than a jeweller's bench, with a sandbag to raise the work up. Good lighting and a loupe or magnifying glass are essential.

The graver is held with the handle in the palm of the hand and with the thumb and index finger extended along the graver. Forward pressure from the hand pushes the graver along, removing slivers of metal as it slides forwards, the movement comes from the wrist. Attention should be paid to the angle that the graver is held at; if it is too high, the tip may dig in to the surface, stopping the graver moving forwards easily. But if it's held too low, the graver may slip.

Curved lines are usually cut anti-clockwise, with the supporting hand turning the work into the path of the graver as it cuts. Textures are created by a side-to-side rocking action as the graver moves forwards.

Unwanted marks on the surface can be removed by rubbing a burnisher along the line rather than across it; this pushes the metal from the sides of the line into the groove. You may also need to use emery paper. Soldering and other finishing carried out after engraving may cause the bright cut of the incised lines to disappear, but this can be returned by careful polishing.

An understanding of the subtle changes of pressure, angle and tilt of the graver are essential for successful results, and daily practice on off-cuts of silver is recommended before engraving a finished piece. Master straight lines first, before moving on to curves and textures.

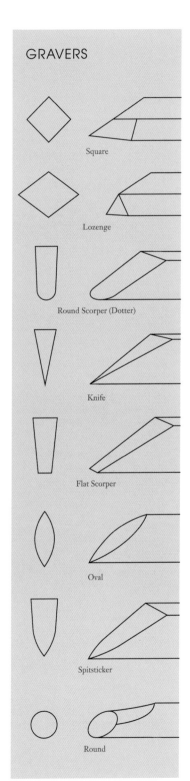

GRAVERS

Square

Lozenge

Round Scorper (Dotter)

Knife

Flat Scorper

Oval

Spitsticker

Round

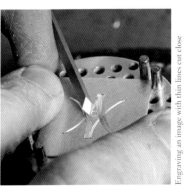

Engraving an image with thin lines cut close together (threading) using a square graver.

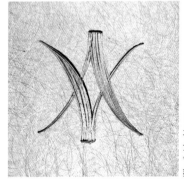

The finished image.

ENGRAVING TUTORIAL

by Steven North

YOU WILL NEED

- Silver sheet
- Engraver's vice
- Sandbag
- Square, flat scorper, dotter (half-round) gravers
- Plasticine and French chalk
- Pointed wooden or plastic marking tool
- Scriber
- Dividers
- Oilstone and Arkansas stone
- Three-in-one oil
- Loupe or magnifying glass
- Burnisher
- Emery paper

THE PROCESS

1. Mount a piece of sterling silver sheet with a fine papered finish in an engraver's vice, and then place it on a sandbag. Mark the lines on to the metal by rolling plasticine over the surface, dusting with French chalk and then drawing the lines on with a pointed wooden tool, followed by dividers and a scriber.

2. Use a square graver to cut a straight line. Hold this firmly with the handle of the graver sat in the palm of your hand and your thumb and index finger extended along the length of the graver. Press the tip of the graver down into the metal at the start of the line, then lower the angle of the graver and push it forwards as far as can be accomplished in one go. Flick the sliver of metal that was removed by the graver out at the end of the cut. Widen the thin engraved line by rotating the graver to one side while re-cutting. This type of line creates the appearance of depth.

3. Create a broader line using a wider graver called a flat scorper. Hold the graver and use it in the same way as in Step 2. This type of engraving can be used for block lettering and Roman numerals.

4. Engrave several thin lines side by side using a square graver. Hold the graver and use it in the same way as in Step 2. This technique is called threading.

5. Use a square graver to create a curved line. Hold the graver as before, but this time the supporting hand turns the work into the path of the graver as it cuts, creating a curved line. A faster turn will create a sharper curve. Rotate the graver to one side as it approaches each apex of the curve, returning to its original position afterwards. This widens the cut at the apex, returning to a narrower cut and point as the curve ends. This is called bright cutting.

6. Use a dotter (half-round graver) to create dots. Holding the graver firmly with the handle in the palm of your hand, dig the tip of the graver into the silver and flick it up to remove the metal. This type of mark can be built up over an area to create texture.

1.

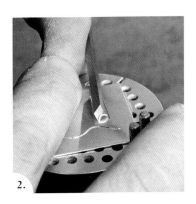

2.

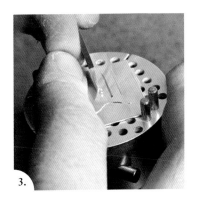

3.

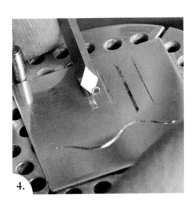

4.

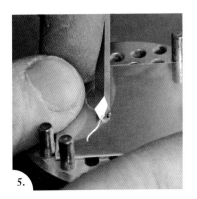

5.

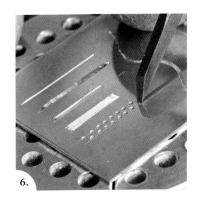

6.

HINTS & TIPS

Beginners will usually need to cut a longer line in several sections. These sections should all be cut at the same depth and angle so that they blend into each other. Making a longer cut in one continuous action comes with experience.

Make sure that engraved lines are deep enough so that they do not disappear if the piece is rubbed with emery paper or given a polished finish.

A zigzag texture or wriggled line is fairly easy to make by rocking the graver from side to side as it is pushed forwards. The effect created will depend upon the angle of the graver, the speed and action of the wrist movement and the pressure applied. Flat or rounded gravers can be used.

A sharp graver will create a cut with very little burr. Keep tools sharpened and lubricate the tip of the graver while working by dabbing it on some absorbent cotton that has been saturated with wintergreen or mineral oil.

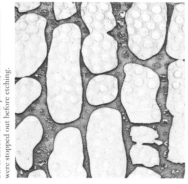

Silver sheet was roller printed, then selected areas were stopped out before etching.

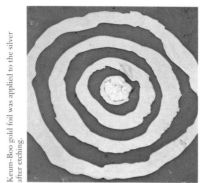

Keum-Boo gold foil was applied to the silver after etching.

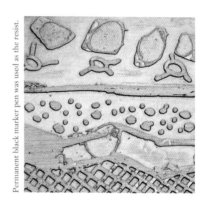

Permanent black marker pen was used as the resist.

ETCHING

Etching is the technique of corroding away metal using acid to create areas of varying depth below the surface. The acid is often referred to as a mordant. The process involves applying a resist to the metal to mask off areas, leaving the exposed metal to be eaten by the acid. Etching can produce a range of different effects that are dependent upon the type of resist and its method of application, the strength of the acid solution and the careful timing of the etching process. It can be used to provide recesses for inlay and colour, to create pattern and texture on a sheet of silver that is then fabricated and formed and can also be used on surfaces of already-fabricated pieces. Consideration should be given to the depth of etch required and the thickness of the silver used.

ETCHING TECHNIQUE

Silver can be etched using either one part nitric acid to three parts water, or one part ferric nitrate to three parts distilled warm water. Nitric acid, also known as aquafortis, is dangerous and must be used very carefully, following health and safety guidelines. Ferric nitrate (used for the tutorial in this book) comes in crystal form, and, although it is not a pure acid, it is corrosive and poisonous. It produces a slower etch time, but is a safer option because it does not give off as many fumes as nitric acid. However, the warmed solution gives off a vapour that should not be inhaled. Health and safety procedures should always be followed, ferric nitrate can stain skin and clothes so adequate protection should be worn.

Both nitric acid and ferric nitrate should be mixed within a fume cupboard and in a glass container, such as a Pyrex dish. Latex or rubber gloves and eye protection must be worn. If a fume cupboard is not available, then a well-ventilated area must be used and a respirator mask worn to filter the fumes. Acid should *always* be added to water, *never* water to acid. Acid that has already been used increases in strength until it becomes saturated with the metal that it has eaten away. Mixed acid solutions should be stored in clearly labelled and well-sealed glass bottles. It is also important to follow proper disposal procedures for spent acids.

A number of resists can be used to mask off areas of the metal to prevent the acid from etching it away. For etching silver with nitric acid or ferric nitrate, any of the following resists can be used: stop-out varnish, oil-based printmaker's varnish (sometimes called black polish), brown plastic waterproof parcel tape, plastic stickers and Press 'n' Peel paper (PnP). In addition to this, ferric nitrate will also resist permanent marker pen and nail varnish.

Before applying a resist, the metal should be cleaned and completely degreased; if the resist does not adhere to the surface, then it might lift off during the etching process. A surface finish can be given to the silver before applying the resist. Both stop-out varnish and nail varnish can be applied with a brush or sponge. Painting the entire surface with the resist allows a design to be drawn into it/scratched through to expose the metal underneath. Different levels can be created by removing the silver from the solution partway through the etching process and painting the resist on to some of the already-etched areas, or by firstly etching areas of a design that are to be the deepest, then removing the piece from the solution and exposing more areas of the silver by scratching the design from the resist, so that each time the piece is returned to the solution the first area will etch deeper.

PnP paper is an acetate sheet coated with a blue film that forms the resist and is usually used to create copper circuit boards. Fairly accurate depictions of images can be produced using a type of low-tech photo-etching technique by transferring high-contrast black-and-white images or text on to silver using a photocopier, PnP paper and heat. If the image needs to be reversed, it is first printed on to acetate, then printed on to the matte side of the PnP paper. This is then transferred on to the silver using a household iron. Using a high-contrast image can give strikingly detailed results on the silver.

During the etching process, bubbles can form on the surface of the metal preventing it from etching properly and causing an uneven bite. This is more likely to occur when using a nitric acid solution. These bubbles should be removed by gently brushing the silver with a feather. A slow etch is better than a fast etch, as a fast etch causes an aggressive bite, which creates uneven results and can cause the resist to lift away.

The surface of an etched piece can be left as it is once the resist has been removed, or it can be scrubbed with wire wool, finished with emery paper or pumice powder, etc. Other techniques such as texturing, colouring and gold leafing can be combined successfully with etching to enhance the results.

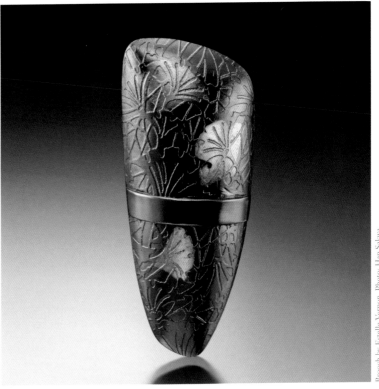

Brooch by Estelle Vernon. Photo: Hap Sakwa.

ETCHING TUTORIAL

Etching and Photo Etching by *Melissa Hunt*

YOU WILL NEED

- Silver sheet
- Electric hotplate
- Heat-resistant glass container
- Glass jar or oversized lid if not using a fume cupboard
- Plastic spoon
- Distilled water
- Ferric nitrate/iron nitrate
- Stop-out varnish/nail varnish
- Permanent black marker pens
- Plastic stickers
- Brown plastic parcel tape
- Brushes
- Scriber
- Sponge
- Plastic or brass rod
- Garden wire
- Latex or rubber gloves
- Mask and safety glasses
- Plastic tweezers
- Methyl hydrate/denatured alcohol (methylated spirit)
- Acetone

THE PROCESS: ETCHING

1. Prepare the solution in a well-ventilated area while wearing safety glasses, a mask, an apron and gloves. Add one part ferric nitrate crystals to three parts distilled water in a glass jar and stir the solution with a plastic spoon. Part fill a heat-resistant glass container with warm water and place it on an electric hotplate, set at a medium temperature. Carefully place the jar with the ferric nitrate solution in the container of water.

2. Prepare and degrease the surface of the silver with denatured alcohol. Place plastic stickers on to the sheet using a craft knife, press each sticker down to make sure it properly adheres to the metal. Cover the back of the silver sheet in plastic parcel tape and fold this over double along two sides. Protect the edges of the silver sheet from etching away by carefully painting them with nail varnish.

3. Using a scriber, make a hole through the parcel tape halfway along one of the doubled-over sides. Make a loop in one end of a piece of plastic garden wire and pass the other end through the hole in the parcel tape and secure it. Use a brass rod to suspend the silver and then carefully lower the piece into the ferric nitrate solution. Place an oversized lid over the jar to contain the vapour.

4. Keep the hotplate at a low-to-medium temperature to ensure a slow etch. Stir the solution occasionally with a plastic spoon to prevent sediment building up at the bottom. Check the progress of the etching regularly by removing the piece from the solution, rinsing it in cold water, then carefully using a scriber or pin to check the depth of etch.

5. When the etch is deep enough, rinse the piece well and remove the stickers. Remove the nail varnish using a paper towel and acetone.

6. After preparing and degreasing the surface of a piece of silver sheet, use a permanent black marker pen to mask off areas. Apply plastic parcel tape to the back and then use the marker pen to mask the edges of the silver sheet to protect these from being etched away.

7. Etch the piece for one to two hours. Once a deep enough etch has been achieved, rinse the piece well and remove the marker pen with a paper towel and denatured alcohol.

1.

2.

3.

4.

6.

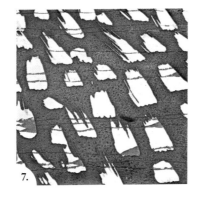

7.

HINTS & TIPS

The edges of the silver may etch away, despite being painted with the resist. Use a larger sheet of silver than required and cut to size after etching to compensate for this.

Stop-out areas of a piece that do not require etching, such as the back of a flat sheet and the inside of a ring, paying particular attention to edges.

Do not apply stop-out varnish too thinly because it may peel away in the etching solution. If the resist lifts away, rinse and thoroughly dry the piece, then reapply the stop-out to the area.

Always add acid (or ferric nitrate crystals) to water, never the other way round.

ETCHING TUTORIAL

Etching and Photo Etching Continued by Melissa Hunt

FOR THE PHOTO ETCHING

- High-contrast black-and-white image
- Paper
- Acetate sheet
- Press 'n' Peel paper (PnP)
- Photocopier
- Household iron

8. Prepare and degrease the surface of a piece of silver sheet, then apply plastic parcel tape to the back and apply stop-out varnish using a sponge. Allow the varnish to dry fully before placing in the etching solution.

9. Slowly etch the piece for about two hours. When a deep enough etch has been achieved, rinse the piece well and remove the stop-out varnish using a paper towel and acetone.

10. Prepare and degrease the surface of a piece of silver sheet, apply plastic parcel tape to the back, then paint the entire front surface with stop-out varnish. Once the varnish is thoroughly dry, scratch some areas away using a scriber.

THE PROCESS: PHOTO ETCHING

11. Photocopy an image on to white paper, making sure that the print is very black to ensure an image with high contrast. Then photocopy the black-and-white image on to acetate sheet so that it can be reversed before copying on to the dull side of the PnP paper.

12. Cut the image from the PnP paper. Prepare the silver sheet using emery paper and then degrease it with denatured alcohol. Place the PnP paper image-side down on the silver sheet, and, working on a block of wood for insulation with a sheet of paper on top of the silver, apply the image using a medium–hot iron without steam. Use gentle pressure and move the iron slowly over the entire area, taking care not to move the PnP paper.

13. After allowing the silver to cool, carefully peel the PnP paper back from one corner, checking that the ink has applied to the metal. Any areas where the ink has not applied properly can be touched up using a permanent black marker pen.

14. Place parcel tape over the back of the silver and fold it in to cover the edges. Make a hole in one side of the tape and attach plastic garden wire. Etch the piece slowly for about five hours, stirring the ferric nitrate solution occasionally and checking the depth regularly.

15. After removing it from the solution, rinse and dry the piece well. Remove the resist using a paper towel and acetone, and cut the silver to size.

8.

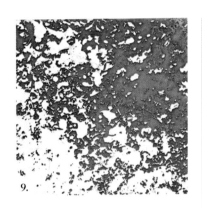

9.

10.

11.

12.

13.

HINTS & TIPS

The silver should be completely covered by the etching solution. If several pieces are being etched in the same solution at the same time, make sure that each piece has its own space and is not resting against another.

A slow etch is better than a fast etch.

Stir the ferric nitrate solution occasionally to prevent sediment settling on the bottom and check the depth of etch regularly with a pin or scriber.

Acid can be neutralised with bicarbonate of soda. Mix it to a paste with water before applying it to the metal.

Rings by Shimara Carlow. Photo: Keith Leighton.

Ring by Shimara Carlow. Photo: Keith Leighton.

Earrings by Estelle Vernon. Photo: Jessica Marcotte.

RETICULATION

Reticulation is the texturing of metal by controlled heat to produce a unique raised and wrinkled effect. The results are unpredictable and depend somewhat on practice and serendipity, consequently it is not possible to repeat exactly the same effect more than once.

MATERIALS FOR RETICULATION

Reticulation relies on the different melting points and cooling rates of metal alloys. The wrinkles created from reticulation appear to have taken place on the surface, when in actual fact all the movement takes place underneath, where the interior of the silver melts prior to the surface melting. For this to happen the sterling silver must be depletion gilded; during this process the surface is stripped of its copper content and replaced by a fine silver layer. This creates the different melting points and cooling rates between the interior and the exterior that are essential for reticulation.

Sterling silver, which consists of 92.5% fine silver and 7.5% copper works well, however, a higher copper content will produce more dramatic results. Some suppliers offer reticulation silver alloys of 80–83% fine silver and 20–17% copper. (Note that the lower silver content means that it cannot be hallmarked. See page 188 for more information about hallmarking.)

The thickness of the sheet used will affect the outcome of the texture; if the silver is too thin, holes are more likely to develop. 18-gauge (1.0mm) or thicker is a safe choice. Using a larger piece of silver than required is recommended because the sheet will shrink as the edges distort and pull in during the process. The most interesting and successful areas can be cut from the reticulated sheet for use afterwards.

RETICULATION PROCESS

To produce a fine silver surface, the depletion gilding process of annealing, pickling and cleaning is repeated seven times. Preheating a charcoal block with a torch prior to reticulating helps the silver maintain an even heat during the process. A large, bushy flame is used to heat the silver beyond annealing temperature, causing the interior to reach melting point. A finer pointed flame is created and passed over an area and then quickly moved on. It is at this moment that the cooling causes the interior to contract, and in turn creates the surface distortion. Two torches can be used together,

one maintaining the temperature with a large bushy flame; the second finer and more pointed flame is introduced once the silver is red-hot. The second flame is used to create the texture, while the bushy flame maintains the temperature.

The surface should be carefully observed as holding the second flame for too long in one place can create holes. Adding fine silver pieces (wire or jump rings), to the surface will enhance the effects. Controlling the direction of the flame over the surface will result in specific areas becoming textured, rather than the whole piece.

Reticulated silver is brittle and should be annealed before any further forming takes place. Forming the sheet prior to reticulating is possible, but it will be at a greater risk of its shape distorting or holes developing because, unlike a flat sheet, it cannot be completely supported from behind.

Practice is highly recommended to gain confidence with this technique.

Necklace by Shinara Carlow. Photo: Keith Leighton.

RETICULATION TUTORIAL

Reticulating Sterling Silver Sheet by *Michael Milloy*

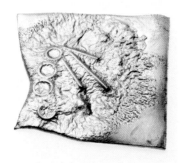

YOU WILL NEED

- Sterling silver sheet 18-gauge (1.0mm) minimum thickness
- Fine silver jump rings and wire
- Charcoal block
- Torch
- Steel tweezers
- Pumice powder
- Brass brush
- Liquid soap
- Pickling solution

THE PROCESS

1. Depletion gild a piece of 18-gauge (1.0mm) sterling silver sheet (see page 117 for information about depletion gilding).

2. Pre-heat the charcoal block to help the silver retain an even temperature throughout the process.

3. Place the silver on the charcoal block and heat it to beyond annealing temperature with a large flame.

4. Play a sharper flame over an area of the silver sheet and, once movement is observed, swifly pull the flame back. Repeat this over the whole sheet until a satisfactory effect has been achieved.

5. To enhance the effects, add fine silver jump rings and wire to the surface of the sterling silver during the heating process.

6. Allow the piece to cool for a short while on the charcoal block before quenching, pickling and then cleaning with a brass brush and liquid soap.

7. Cut up a larger sheet of reticulated silver so that the most successful area can be used.

2.

3.

4.

5.

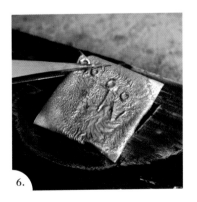

6.

7.

HINTS & TIPS

Because of shrinkage and distortion, start with a larger piece of silver than needed, then cut and use the most successful areas from this. The thickness of the finished sheet may vary.

Make sure the charcoal block is very flat so that it supports the sheet.

Change the angle of the torch as it works over the surface.

Anneal before further forming.

The reticulated sheet can be flattened with a mallet or passed through a rolling mill.

If you use reticulation silver, label it and keep it separate from sterling.

Check hallmarking regulations when using reticulation silver in combination with sterling, because it has less silver and more copper.

Oxidising works well with reticulation because it helps add definition to the texture.

Okano cuff by Christy Klug. Photo: Ralph Gabriner.

Ring by Daphne Krinos. Photo: Joel Degen.

Cuff by Todd Reed. Photo: Craig Pratt.

OXIDISING AND COLOURING

Silver can be coloured by the controlled use of both chemicals and heat. These colouring processes work particularly well when the surface has recesses or texture because the colour helps to create depth and highlight detail, especially when combined with areas that have not received colour or had the colour removed from them. Restricting the colour to a particular part or using it next to another metal such as gold will create striking contrasts.

The colouring processes are surface treatments, so they may not be durable enough for pieces of jewellery that receive a certain amount of wear and tear such as rings, because the colour will eventually wear away over time. Colouring textured silver and then using abrasives to remove the colour from raised surface areas, leaving it in any recesses, helps alleviate this problem.

Colouring should be done after all fabrication and finishing has taken place. The surface finish given to the silver directly affects the colour, for example, a matte finish produces a more intense colour. The silver must be cleaned and degreased before colouring.

All chemical colouring must be carried out in a well-ventilated area, fume cupboard or outdoors. A mask, apron and latex gloves should be worn and plenty of water made available.

OXIDISING SILVER

The chemical oxidising of silver is carried out using a warm liver of sulphur solution and re-creates the tarnishing effects that naturally occur when silver is exposed to the atmosphere. The solution is made by dissolving a very small piece of potassium sulphide (available in lump form), in 100ml (3fl oz) of warm water, or by mixing 25ml (1fl oz) of a commercial oxidising solution (known as liver of sulphur or ammonium hydro-sulphide) to 1l (1qt) of water and heating to 60–70°C (145–160°F). The solution has a strong, unpleasant smell. If it's not possible to heat the liver of sulphur solution, the silver itself can be heated by placing it in a container of hot water. The metal is oxidised by immersing it in the liver of sulphur solution for about 20 seconds, it is then thoroughly rinsed in cold water.

You can produce an antiqued effect by using an abrasive to remove some of the colour from the surface, leaving recessed areas oxidised and dark. In addition to dark grey and black, a surprisingly wide range of other colours can be obtained, such as yellows, red/pinks, blue/purples and browns, by using the liver of sulphur solution as it cools and monitoring the development in colour changes. Remove the silver from the solution once the desired colour is reached. However, it can be difficult to repeat the exact same colour again.

Applying a microcrystalline wax to an oxidised piece protects and darkens the colour. When the silver has been in contact with the oxidising solution for a short time and the result is a colour that is not dark grey or black, apply wax with caution to a test area first. These colours can be more vulnerable to undesirable colour changes through the application of the wax.

Platinol is a commercial concentrated oxidisation chemical that produces a grey to black colour and does not require heat. It is applied with a synthetic brush to specific areas; repeated applications will darken the colour. After rinsing and drying, applying a micro-crystalline wax darkens the colour further and helps to protect it.

For chemical-free oxidising, silver can be placed in a Ziploc bag with half a hot, hard-boiled egg. Seal the bag and leave for a day or two so that the egg fumes oxidise the silver.

COPPER PLATING

Copper plating textured silver can be effective, especially when the copper colour is removed from a raised surface area, leaving it in the recesses where it is less vulnerable to wear and tear. To copper plate silver, iron binding wire is placed in a warm pickling solution, together with the silver. The binding wire can be wrapped around the silver to help speed up the process and to develop a thicker deposit. Introducing small copper pieces to the pickling solution, especially if it is new, will also help. Unlike the oxidised silver, the copper areas are vulnerable to tarnishing, so the overall effect will change over time.

HEAT COLOURING

Sterling silver can also be coloured by passing a gentle flame over the metal and monitoring the development in colour changes. When the desired colour has been reached, quickly remove the flame. Pickling will completely remove the

colour and should therefore be avoided. The results rely on chance and the surface can be easily marked.

Depletion gilding can be used to create a frosty white colour. The silver is gently and evenly heated, then quenched in a freshly-made warm pickling solution. The process is repeated up to seven times or until the silver has stopped oxidising and there is a clean, white silver-rich surface. This surface is susceptible to marks and scratches, so can be used to great effect by creating a contrasting surface finish on areas that will receive wear and tear. Before quenching the silver in a warm pickling solution, the metal should be allowed to cool for a little on the fire brick and care should be taken not to splash the hot pickle on clothes and skin.

Flower brooches by Kate Hodgson. Photo: Full Focus.

OXIDISING AND COLOURING TUTORIAL

Copper Plating, Oxidising with Liver of Sulphur and Oxidising with Platinol

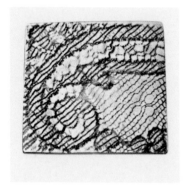

YOU WILL NEED

FOR COPPER PLATING

- Textured silver sheet
- Warm pickle
- Glass jar
- Plastic tweezers
- Iron binding wire
- Small pieces of copper
- Water
- Emery paper

FOR OXIDISING

- Silver sheet and textured silver sheet
- Liver of sulphur and Platinol
- Water
- Heat-proof glass container
- Hotplate
- Plastic tweezers
- Synthetic-bristled paintbrush
- Latex gloves
- Mask
- Apron
- Microcrystalline wax
- Clean soft cloth

THE PROCESS: COPPER PLATING

1. Clean and degrease a textured piece of silver. Transfer some warm pickle solution to a glass jar. Cut some small pieces of copper, and wrap the iron binding wire around the clean silver.

2. Place the copper pieces in the warm pickle and immerse the silver.

3. Check the progress of the plating regularly. Once there is enough of a copper deposit on the silver, remove it, then rinse and dry it.

4. Use a fine emery paper over the surface to reveal the silver, leaving the copper in the recesses.

1.

2.

3.

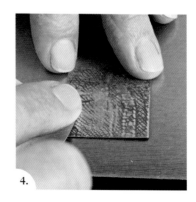

4.

THE PROCESS: OXIDISING WITH LIVER OF SULPHUR

5. Clean and degrease the silver with pumice powder and a brush, followed by liquid soap and hot water. Rinse and dry it.

6. Add 25ml (1fl oz) of liver of sulphur to 1l (1qt) of water and heat to 60–70°C (145–160°F). Immerse the silver in the warm solution for about 20 seconds, or until the desired colour has been reached.

7. After rinsing and drying, create a scratched and light grey surface with pumice powder and a brass brush. Apply microcrystalline wax to the surface with a soft cloth.

8. Clean and degrease a roller-printed piece of silver, then dip it in and out of a lukewarm liver of sulphur solution until the desired colours are reached. Rinse and dry it.

9. Carefully rub a fine emery paper over the surface to reveal the silver, leaving the colours in the recesses.

THE PROCESS: OXIDISING WITH PLATINOL

10. Clean a piece of silver with shapes or recesses using a brass pencil brush, then apply Platinol using a synthetic-bristled paintbrush.

11. After rinsing and drying, apply microcrystalline wax to protect and darken the colour.

HINTS & TIPS

Make sure that any solder is cleaned off well before oxidising as this may cause colour variations.

If the liver of sulphur solution is too strong or the Platinol applied too thickly, the oxidised layer can peel.

Use nail varnish to mask off areas before applying Platinol.

Monitor the colouring progress regularly, some colours require longer than others to develop.

Results from colouring can vary, so experiment on pieces of scrap silver before colouring a final piece. To remove an unwanted colour, anneal and pickle or use abrasives.

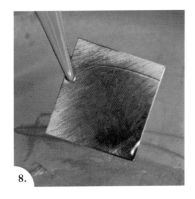

8.

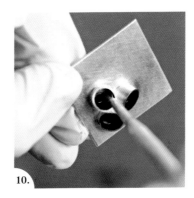

10.

11.

FINISHING SURFACES

Finishing generally refers to the removal of scratches and marks, as well as the nature of the final surface finish, such as satin/matte or polished. The type of finish given can transform a piece, so it is important to plan the finishing before and during the fabrication stages. While in most situations finishing will be the final step, there will be instances where a piece may need to have the surfaces of some parts finished or taken to a certain stage of finishing before joining to others, particularly where it may be hard to reach an area once it has been attached or assembled.

Surface finishes change with wear and tear; the degree to which this happens depends on the type of piece and how vulnerable it is when worn – a ring or bangle will receive more wear and tear than a necklace or pair of earrings, for example. Satin and matte surfaces are more porous than polished ones and fingerprint marks are also more noticeable on them.

FINISHING STAGES

Silver is a relatively soft metal, making it susceptible to marking. The finishing steps should start with using a file to remove solder and any marks left by tools. Papering or sanding the surface with emery or wet and dry paper is the next stage to remove firescale and scratches. It is important that the various stages required to remove the scratches are worked through; deep scratches are removed by replacing them with finer ones until a fine satin or mirror-like surface has been reached. Each grade of paper should be used in a different direction to the last so that the mark removal can be seen. Creating a satin or matte surface requires the same steps to be worked through as for a polished surface – taking the metal to the final stage before polishing to ensure that all deep scratches are removed, and then taking the surface back to the desired satin or matte finish.

ABRASIVES

Both emery and wet and dry papers are available in a range of grades from coarse to fine. They can be applied to various-shaped wooden sticks with double-sided tape or glue, used by hand in small pieces and as flat sheets, as well as with a split pin in a pendant motor to clean up inside rings, etc. A matte or satin silver surface can sometimes look a little dull and can be brightened by using a brass brush with liquid soap as a final stage. Other abrasives include: steel wool, Scotch-Brite, impregnated flexible abrasive blocks, pumice powder (available in several grades) and brass and glass brushes. Using the pendant motor speeds up the finishing process and there are a wide variety of abrasives and texturing tools available as attachments including steel burrs; carborundum abrasives; silicone rubber wheels; steel, brass, and bristle pendant brushes and frosting wheels.

POLISHING

This can be done by hand or using a buffing machine, pendant motor or a barrel polisher. Polishing by hand is suitable for small areas or very delicate pieces and can be done with a polishing cream applied with a soft clean cloth, or using leather that has been glued to wooden sticks and then had tripoli rouge applied to it. Polishing strings are useful for hard-to-reach areas. A steel burnisher can be used to polish or burnish details and edges by hand, but the grades of abrasive paper must be worked through first.

Machine polishing is quicker and is carried out using polishing mops that attach to a rotating spindle on a buffing machine. The polishing compounds used for silver are tripoli (dark brown), used first on a stiff mop to remove fine scratches, followed by rouge (red) with a softer mop. Each mop should be used with one compound only. Machine polishing must be carried out with care while wearing safety glasses and a dust mask, long hair should be tied back and loose items of clothing rolled up. Only the lower quarter of the wheel should be used and both hands used to grip the work; if the piece catches and is snatched away, release your grip immediately and switch the machine off before retrieving it. The piece should be washed in hot soapy water or in an ultrasonic cleaner between using each different polish. Certain items should not be polished by machine, such as chains, because these are easily snatched away. There are numerous pendant motor polishing attachments that can be used with tripoli and rouge for polishing hard-to-reach areas.

Tumbling is carried out using a rotating drum called a barrel polisher containing steel shot in various shapes and sizes and a lubricant of water and soap, or a commercial solution. Tumbling will polish or burnish and also work harden, but it does not remove metal like an abrasive will. Chains should be polished in a tumbler, not on a buffing machine. Pieces that are particularly delicate or have stones should not be tumbled.

DEPLETION GILDING AND FIRESCALE REMOVAL

This process is similar to plating and is usually used to remove the formation of firescale on sterling silver. After giving the surface its final finish, the sterling silver is heated so that the copper in the surface of the alloy oxidises. This oxidised copper layer is removed by quenching in a freshly-made, hot pickling solution (depletion). This process deposits a layer of fine silver on the surface (gilding) that appears as a frosty, clean, white colour. The heating and quenching process is repeated five to seven times and each time there is noticeably less oxidation on the surface until finally there is none at all. The resulting white silver surface is susceptible to marks and scratches from wear and tear, making the process ideal for use on pieces with recesses where these areas will not come in to constant contact with anything that may mark them. It can be used to great effect by creating a contrasting surface finish on those areas that will receive wear and tear. The surface can also be finished with a brass brush and soap.

Safety precautions should be taken when using this method; before quenching the silver in a hot pickling solution, the metal should be allowed to cool on the fire brick and care should be taken not to splash hot pickle on clothes and skin.

DEGREASING SILVER

Techniques such as colouring and etching require the surface to be properly cleaned and degreased. Wear latex gloves to avoid the surface coming into contact with your fingers. Scrub the silver using pumice powder and a brush or use a glass brush under water to contain the fibres and prevent them from penetrating the skin. Water will form a complete film over the metal if it is grease free. Using denatured alcohol (methylated spirit) will also degrease the metal, but where there are recesses in the surface, the first method is more efficient.

FINISHING SURFACES TUTORIAL

YOU WILL NEED

- Coarse to fine grades of emery or wet and dry papers
- Steel block or flat clean surface
- Emery sticks
- Brass brush
- Pumice powder
- Scotch-Bite and/or wire wool
- Polishing machine
- Two polishing mops
- Tripoli and rouge polishing compounds
- Various pendant motor attachments: steel burrs, spilt pin, mops, etc.
- Burnisher
- Burr lube and three-in-one oil
- Various silver pieces to finish
- Finger protection

THE PROCESS

1. To remove file marks, use a medium and then a finer grade emery paper stick, working in a different direction to the marks created by the file. Finish flat edges using various grades of emery paper placed on a steel flat plate, completing the papering action in a figure of eight pattern on the finest grade to give an even finish. Apply the final surface finish with Scotch-Brite.

2. To use a split pin with emery paper in a pendant motor, cut a long strip of emery paper and place it in the slot of the split pin, winding it around tightly. Support the hand holding the piece against the bench peg and protect your fingers with rubber finger cots. When cleaning a ring or bangle, use the split pin from both sides of the piece to ensure an even finish. As the paper becomes worn, cut it back to reveal new paper.

3. To give a piece a polished finish using a mop and polishing motor, work through the grades of emery paper, then polish the piece with tripoli on a stiff mop, followed with rouge on a softer mop. Working on the lower quarter of the mop, apply the polishing compound, then use both hands to hold the piece and guide it in and out of the spinning mop. Use your secondary hand to support the primary hand during some of the polishing movements.

4. To create two different finishes on one piece, first work through the grades of emery paper from coarse to fine to remove marks and leave a semi-polished surface. Polish one section using leather glued to a stick with tripoli or rouge applied to it, or use a buffing machine. Wash any polish away with hot soapy water or place the piece in an ultrasonic cleaner. Cover the polished surface with masking tape to protect the finish. Give the other section a matte surface finish by hand, using a small, circular and even rubbing action with emery paper.

5. To recreate the texture or surface after removing a sprue from a cast piece, use a steel burr in a pendant motor. Support the hand holding the piece against the bench peg and protect your fingers with rubber finger cots.

6. Create different surface textures using various steel burrs in a pendant motor. Use plenty of lubrication and keep the burr moving over the surface to build up the texture.

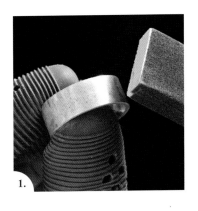

1.

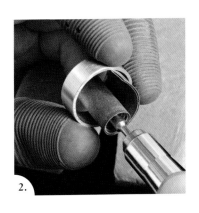

2.

3.

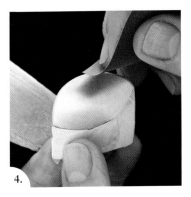

4.

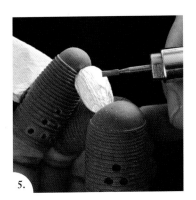

5.

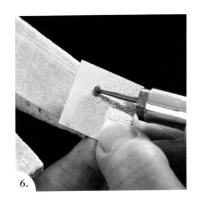

6.

HINTS & TIPS

Use a little three-in-one oil when burnishing and cut lube with steel burrs in the pendant motor to prolong the life of burrs and help with texturing.

Firescale can be removed using a Water of Ayr stone. Keep the stone wet and rub away at the affected areas, rinsing and inspecting the piece regularly.

Surfaces that have been depletion gilded can be given a finish with fine paper, wire wool, brass brush, etc. They don't have to be left with a white frosty surface.

Concentration is vital when using a buffing machine. Make sure that your fingers are not trapped in the work so they can easily be released if necessary. Long hair should be tied back and loose items of clothing, such as sleeves, rolled up.

Overpolishing can result in a loss of detail and definition, particularly on corners and edges.

Not So Square pendant by Jane Macintosh. Photo: Joël Degen.

Wedding rings by Jörg Egginmann. Photo: Jörg Egginmann.

Silver and gold cluster pendant by Catherine Hills. Photo: Norman Hollands.

MARRIED METALS

Silver can be used in combination with other precious and non-precious metals to add colour, pattern and texture, offering the designer endless creative possibilities. Precious metals are an obvious first choice to work with, but these can be expensive. Non-precious metals such as copper or bronze are good alternatives and also reduce the overall cost. Be sure to check hallmarking regulations when using combinations of different metals.

MARRIED METALS TECHNIQUES

INLAY

Inlay describes the surface of the metal when it has had contrasting metals laid or secured into it. The result is a flat surface with colour and pattern differences, which looks like one piece of metal. Traditional inlay uses chisels to gouge out a recess in the metal. The recess is then filled with wire or sheet that is tapped into place using hammers and tools. There are five different inlay techniques.

Applied Inlay: A technique where the metal to be inlaid is appliquéd or joined to the surface of the parent metal by soldering. It is then passed through a rolling mill until the appliquéd metal becomes flush with the base metal.

Piqué Work: Popular in seventeenth and eighteenth century France, this is a technique of inlaying small gold pins into tortoiseshell. Dotted patterns can be created in silver by soldering a contrasting metal wire into a drilled hole.

Solder Inlay: In this technique, solder is flooded into grooves in the silver. The grooves can be made with hammers, punches, roller printing, engraving or etching.

Jigsaw/Puzzle Inlay: As the name suggests, this technique involves cutting pieces that fit together like a jigsaw puzzle and then soldering them. The advantage of this process is that the inlay can be seen on both the front and the back of the piece.

Lamination Inlay: A pattern is pierced from one piece of metal and then soldered or laminated to another. The laminate is compressed until both sheets are flush.

OVERLAY

Overlay describes the surface of the metal when it has had contrasting metals applied to it to create a pattern. The overlay can be built up piece-by-piece using contrasting textures and coloured metals, or it can be done by cutting patterns out of pieces.

FUSING

With this technique, two pieces of metal are welded together by heating them to their melting points, thus eliminating the need for solder. Fusing has a multitude of creative possibilities and is a useful technique for using up pieces of scrap and gold dust. However, the process can be unpredictable and difficult to control, and so should be avoided if precision is needed.

KEUM-BOO/KUM-BU (ATTACHED GOLD)

An ancient Korean technique where 24-carat gold foil is applied to silver using heat and pressure. Keum-Boo foil is thicker than gold leaf and should not be confused with it. Pieces of high-carat gold foil are cut from a thin sheet using a scalpel or scissors and are then applied to a clean silver surface with a damp paintbrush. The silver is then brought to annealing temperature and the gold foil burnished to the surface, where it bonds. When the foil has bonded, the piece can be pickled and lightly finished, and any silver areas that remain uncovered by the foil can be oxidised to enhance the contrast between the silver and the gold foil.

GOLD PLATING

Plating is a thin layer of gold applied to the surface of the metal, using a plating bath and highly toxic chemicals. It should be carried out professionally by a recommended company. The piece should always be completely finished and any stones set before plating takes place. Remember that the gold plate will have the same surface finish as the silver underneath it. The piece should be cleaned and degreased before plating.

ALTERNATIVES

Ready-made married metals are available in several forms, including bi-metal (a layer of gold bonded with sterling silver, also known as two-tone metal and clad metal), mokume-gane, and silver with palladium sprinkles.

Constructed Pod neckpiece by Talya Baharal.
Photo: Gene Gnida.

MARRIED METALS TUTORIAL
Applied Inlay

YOU WILL NEED

- Silver sheet
- Emery paper
- Gold tube
- Tube cutter
- Piercing saw
- Hard silver solder
- Pickling solution
- Torch
- Pumice powder
- Brass brush
- Rolling mill
- Hide mallet
- Steel block
- Oxidising solution
- Microcrystalline wax
- Fire brick/charcoal block
- Flat-hand file

THE PROCESS

1. Prepare a silver sheet by cleaning the surface that will receive the appliqué with emery paper. Cut a piece of 18-carat tube into approximately 2.0mm (⁵⁄₆₄in) lengths using a tube cutter and piercing saw. File the tube flat on one side.

2. Apply flux to the silver sheet and position the tube ready for soldering. Position two small pieces of hard silver solder at opposite sides of the tube so that they sit flat on the silver sheet with one edge touching the gold tube.

3. Introduce the torch with a gentle flame to start with, so as not to disturb the carefully positioned pieces of tube and solder too much. Rectify any movement by nudging the tube and solder back into position with the soldering probe. Keep the flame directly off the tube, and keep it moving as it heats the silver, which in turn will heat the tube. When the solder starts to run, direct the flame to draw the solder flow around the tube.

4. Cool and pickle the piece, then clean it with pumice powder and a brass brush.

5. Gently file the top edges of the tube to level them.

6. Pass the piece through the rolling mill, changing direction on each pass, until the tube becomes flush with the silver sheet. There is unavoidable distortion to the applied metal at this stage.

7. Finish the piece by tapping it flat with a hide mallet on a steel block to rectify any distortion caused by the rollers.

8. Use emery paper to clean up the surface.

9. To highlight the gold and increase the contrast between it and the silver, oxidise and wax the silver.

2.

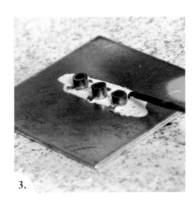

3.

5.

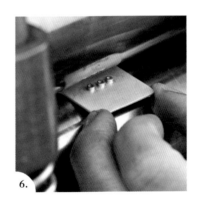

6.

7.

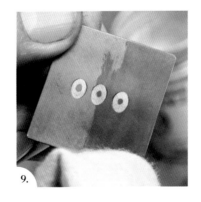

9.

HINTS & TIPS

Experiment with appliquéing wire, rod, sheet, etc. Higher carat gold and copper will have a stronger contrast with the silver, whereas using white gold or palladium will create a subtle contrast.

Increase the surface areas on wires that are to be soldered on by sanding or filing a flat on one side. This makes for a more secure join.

Use binding wire to secure pieces together before soldering.

Make sure the appliquéd piece has soldered on well before passing it through the mill.

If you don't have a mill, use a planishing hammer on the surface until it is flush.

Bear in mind that the rolling mill will cause the final gauge of the metal to be slightly less than what you started out with.

MARRIED METALS TUTORIAL
Piqué Work

YOU WILL NEED

- Marker pen
- Centre punch
- Hammer
- Drill
- Gold wires
- Wire cutters
- Flat/snipe-nose pliers
- Hard and medium
  silver solder
- Flux
- Reverse-action tweezers
- Torch
- Pickling solution
- Piercing saw
- Hand file
- Emery paper
- Drill bits
- Fire brick/charcoal block

THE PROCESS

1. Mark a pattern on your piece with a marker pen and then use a centre punch before drilling holes that are the same diameter as the wire to be used. Make sure that the holes are just deep enough for the wire to sit in securely.

2. File the ends of the wires flat and cut small lengths so that they sit proud once inserted in the holes. The wires need to be a tight fit.

3. Flux the piece, making sure that the flux goes into the holes and then insert a few of the wires.

4. Place small pallions of hard silver solder flat against the silver surface, with one edge resting against the base of the gold wire.

5. Run the solder so that it makes a good join where the wire is inserted into the piece.

6. Once cooled and pickled, cut off the protruding wires with a piercing saw.

7. File the piece so that the gold wires become completely flush with the surface. Remove the file marks with emery paper.

1.

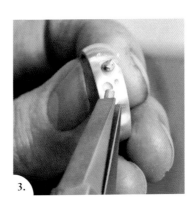

3.

4.

5.

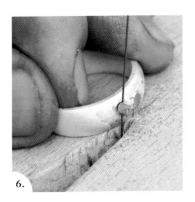

6.

7.

HINTS & TIPS

Drilling a hole creates a burr; use a bud burr in a pendant motor to remove it or file or paper this away before continuing with the rest of the process.

If the wire is too tight to fit in the hole, carefully file the end until it fits.

When cutting off the excess gold wire, collect the dust and offcuts and keep them separate from the silver. These gold scraps can be used for other married metal techniques, such as fusing.

Plan ahead: will there be more joins to be made after the inlay? Start with hard silver solder and try to use this for as many joins as possible. Try to protect previous joins.

MARRIED METALS TUTORIAL
Roller-printed Solder Inlay

YOU WILL NEED

- Silver sheet
- Steel binding wire
- Pliers
- Sticky-back plastic
- Rolling mill
- Brass brush
- Pumice powder
- 18-carat yellow-gold solder
- Pickling solution
- Emery paper
- Oxidising solution
- Fire brick/charcoal block

THE PROCESS

1. Anneal, clean and dry a piece of silver sheet.

2. Bend some steel binding wire into a shape using pliers.

3. Position the wire on the annealed silver sheet and secure it in place with a piece of sticky-back plastic.

4. Pass the sheet and wire through the rolling mill so that an impression is made in the surface of the silver by the steel wire.

5. After cleaning the surface of the silver with a brass brush and pumice powder, flux the recess and place small pieces of easy 18-carat yellow gold solder along it.

6. Heat the piece gently at first, nudging back any solder that moves. Then run the solder into the recess.

7. After cooling and pickling, clean the piece with pumice and a brass brush. Add extra solder if the recess did not receive enough the first time.

8. Sand the surface to remove the excess solder.

9. Apply a fine papered finish to the surface.

10. Finally, oxidise the silver to highlight the inlay.

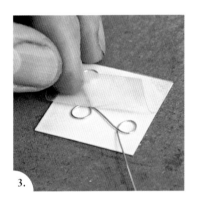

3.

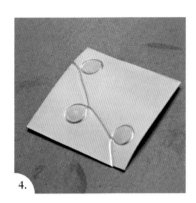

4.

5.

6.

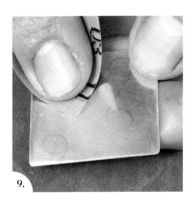

9.

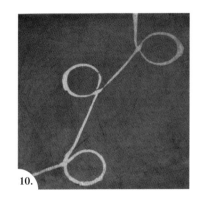

10.

HINTS & TIPS

Make a small test piece to gauge how the rollers should be set to create an impression that is just deep enough to take the solder, but is not too deep. If it's too deep, it will be difficult to fill with the solder.

It is better to cut up smaller pieces of solder that sit well in the recess, rather than use pieces that are too big.

If you don't have sticky-back plastic to secure the wire to the sheet, then wrap the sheet and wire in paper. Do not use sellotape as it easily sticks to the rollers.

Make sure all the sticky-back plastic has been removed before heating.

Plan ahead: if there are to be other joins on the piece, then choose a hard solder for the inlay.

Any of the following will enhance the contrast between the silver and the inlay: a higher carat gold solder, a satin finish or oxidising the silver.

MARRIED METALS TUTORIAL
Jigsaw/Puzzle Inlay

YOU WILL NEED

- Sterling silver sheet
- Gold sheet at the same gauge as the silver sheet
- Scriber
- Hand and needle files
- Piercing saw and blades
- Flat fire brick/charcoal block
- Silver solder
- Torch
- Steel block
- Emery paper

THE PROCESS

1. Mark your design on to the silver sheet with a scriber and cut it out with a piercing saw, then file to neaten it.

2. Place the prepared silver on top of the gold sheet and, using a scriber, mark out the shapes on to the gold. Cut out the gold on the outside of the scribed line, then file it to fit tightly into the silver.

3. Lay the two pieces on a very flat fire brick or charcoal block and flux them on both sides. Place the solder at the bottom corners and, once flowing, use the flame to direct the flow around the shape. If necessary, add extra solder around the join by carefully placing very small pieces where the two metals meet. Turn the piece over and run the solder again to ensure it flows through.

4. After cooling and pickling, cut off the excess gold from the edge and sand the piece flat on a steel block with emery paper.

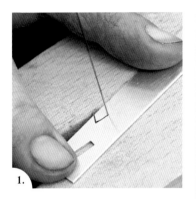

1.

3.

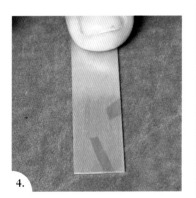

4.

HINTS & TIPS

Make sure that the inlay sheet and the receiving metal are the same gauge.

Both parts of the jigsaw must be a good fit with no gaps. It is better to cut out a piece a little too large and then file it to fit.

An alternative way to cut the shapes is to secure both pieces of metal together with double-sided tape or glue, and cut them in unison.

To inlay a piece where it is necessary to cut from the middle of the receiving metal, drill a small hole and use a piercing saw.

Make sure that the solder does not flow on to the surface of the inlay sheet.

Soldering bricks should be very flat so that the inlay and receiving metal sit at the same level.

Always use silver solder when soldering other metals to silver.

Plan ahead thoroughly when making a married metals piece. If there are going to be multiple solder joins followed by further heating for annealing after work hardening, or perhaps to make other solder joins to complete the piece, then the grades of solder being used need to be thought through before starting.

Some married metals techniques require lots of heat and repeated heating. If you are using sterling silver, remember that firescale can be a problem that arises when too much heat is used for too long.

MARRIED METALS TUTORIAL
Lamination Inlay

YOU WILL NEED

- Sterling silver sheet
- Scriber
- Emery paper
- Pickling solution
- Copper sheet at a thicker gauge than the silver
- Hard silver solder
- Fire brick
- Rolling mill
- Steel plate
- Hide mallet
- Coarse and fine emery paper
- Piercing saw and blades
- Needle files

THE PROCESS

1. Draw a pattern on a piece of sterling silver sheet. Cut out the pattern from the sheet using a piercing saw; first drill a small hole inside each shape, then insert the blade into the hole and cut the shape from the sheet. Refine each one using a needle file.

2. Clean one side of the silver sheet with emery paper, then sweat solder it. Cut up small pallions of solder, flux the sheet and place the pallions on it. Heat and run the solder so that it only just flows.

3. After cooling, pickling and drying, rub the solder across the emery paper to flatten any protruding lumps.

4. Cut a piece of copper sheet that is slightly larger than the silver piece, then clean and flux it. Flux the sweat-soldered silver sheet and place this solder-side down on the copper sheet. Heat and run the solder to join the two together. You should see a shiny silver line running around the outside edge and inside the shapes, confirming that the solder has run.

5. After cooling, pickling and drying well, pass the laminate through the rolling mill, changing direction on each pass. Anneal it each time it becomes work hardened. The process will be complete when the copper sheet has pushed up through the pierced shapes in the silver and the surfaces are flush with each other.

6. Flatten the piece on a steel plate with a hide mallet.

7. Finish the surface using coarse and fine emery paper.

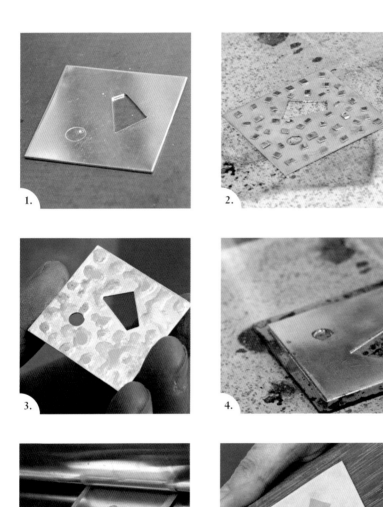

1.

2.

3.

4.

5.

7.

HINTS & TIPS

Make sure that the metal being pushed through the pierced pattern is thicker than the top sheet.

Be aware that the finished sheet will be thinner than the original laminate.

Remember that there will be unavoidable distortion of the pattern. The area on the reverse, where the metal pushes up through the shapes, will also be distorted.

It is important that the solder runs to join the two sheets properly. If you do not observe a shiny silver line running around the outside edges and inside the shapes, introduce additional small pieces of solder to complete the join.

Secure the two sheets with binding wire before soldering to prevent movement.

Make sure the piece is flat before sanding. Secure the piece to a block of wood using double-sided tape.

MARRIED METALS TUTORIAL
Overlay

YOU WILL NEED

- Silver sheet
- Textured copper (or other metal) sheet
- Rectangular or other silver wire
- Emery paper
- Piercing saw and blades
- Hand file
- Hard and medium silver solder
- Pickling solution
- Torch
- Steel tweezers
- Soldering probe
- Pumice powder
- Brass brush
- Hide mallet
- Steel block

THE PROCESS

1. Prepare the copper and silver overlay parts by cutting them to shape and size using a piercing saw, then filing to refine their shape. Where necessary, flatten the sheet on a steel block using a hide mallet.

2. Prepare each part, including the silver parent sheet, for soldering by papering them flat on one side. Assemble the various pieces to check that they are a good fit with no gaps.

3. Flux the overlay pieces and place pallions of solder on the surfaces ready to sweat solder. Heat each piece and run the solder so that it only just flows. After cooling and pickling, gently rub the surfaces on emery paper to flatten them a little, taking care not to remove too much of the solder.

4. Solder the largest overlay piece to the silver parent sheet first. Flux both the parent sheet and the sweat-soldered overlay piece, and place this on top of the parent sheet. Introduce a gentle flame to avoid disturbing the positioning of the overlay piece too much and use tweezers to prevent the piece from moving.

5. Increase the heat and take extra care to prevent the overlay piece becoming hotter than the parent sheet by directing the flame at the charcoal block and the parent sheet. Direct the flow of the solder using the flame; look for a thin shiny line running around the edge of the overlay piece, indicating that the solder has run.

6. After quenching, check the joint, then pickle and clean the piece with pumice powder and a brass brush.

7. Paint flux on to the areas where the next overlay pieces are to be applied to allow these pieces to be soldered on one after the other without pickling in-between. Flux and solder on the next overlay part as in Steps 4 and 5.

8. Continue to solder each overlay part on individually. If the metal becomes too dirty to continue soldering all the pieces, cool, check the joins and then pickle. Clean the piece with pumice powder and a brass brush, then continue to solder the remaining overlay pieces on as before.

9. After cooling, check all the overlay pieces have soldered on properly, then pickle and clean with pumice powder and a brass brush. Clean the join areas using various grades of emery paper; fold the paper so it reaches close into the joins. Use warm soapy water and a small brass brush for a final clean.

2.

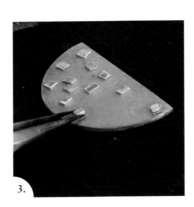

3.

5.

7.

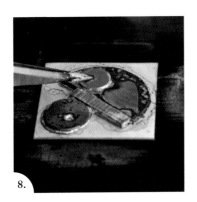

8.

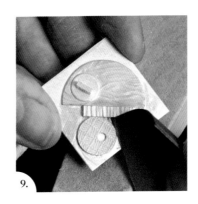

9.

HINTS & TIPS

Make sure that any previous solder joins are not near the area that is to be overlaid, for example a join in a ring.

Check there is good contact between the metals to be joined before sweat soldering.

Apply initial heat to the largest piece, keeping the flame directly off any small pieces.

Make sure you see the solder run, look out for a shiny silver line. If you are unsure, do not pickle the piece because pickle gets drawn into holes and gaps. Cool it in water, then reflux and run it again. Remember to direct the flow of the solder using the flame.

Using the sweat soldering method should produce a neat join that requires very little if any cleaning up. If too much solder is used, the solder can spill out from the join or, if additional pieces of solder have been introduced, these can leave a mark where they were placed. Use a needle file or a burr in a pendant drill to clean the excess solder close to the join. Finish using various grades of emery paper.

MARRIED METALS TUTORIAL

Fusing Gold Pieces to Silver Sheet and Fusing Gold Dust to Silver Sheet

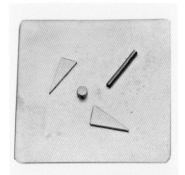

THE PROCESS: FUSING GOLD PIECES TO SILVER SHEET

1. Prepare a piece of silver sheet and pieces of 18 or 22-carat gold sheet and wire by cutting, filing and cleaning them. Assemble the pieces to make sure they are a good fit, with no gaps.

2. Flux the entire surface of one side of the silver sheet and position the gold pieces.

3. Introduce the heat, concentrating it on the base sheet and away from the gold pieces. Once red hot, keep the flame moving over the piece; the silver surface will start to look shiny. At this point, the surface is melting. Take this shiny look across the whole surface, paying particular attention to any pieces of gold that are thicker and require longer to fuse to the silver. Look for a shiny line around each of the gold shapes. At this point, fusing is taking place.

4. Cool the piece and clean it in pickle, followed by pumice and liquid soap, using a brass brush.

YOU WILL NEED

- Silver sheet
- 18 or 22-carat gold scrap and dust
- Piercing saw and blades
- Wire cutters
- Hand and needle files
- Torch
- Pickling solution
- Pumice
- Liquid soap
- Brass brush
- Emery paper
- Rolling mill

2.

3.

THE PROCESS: FUSING GOLD DUST TO SILVER SHEET

5. Clean and flux a piece of silver sheet. Sprinkle gold dust on to the wet flux before it dries out.

6. Repeat Step 3 of the previous tutorial to fuse the dust to the silver sheet.

7. After pickling and a thorough clean with pumice and soap, dry the piece. Anneal the piece so that further work can take place.

8. Fusing metal dust creates a rough surface; to eradicate this, place the piece between two sheets of emery or plain paper, then pass it through a rolling mill once. This compresses the gold dust down, creating a smoother surface as well as an even texture, depending on the type of paper used.

5.

6.

7.

8.

HINTS & TIPS

When using scrap, remove any solder to prevent it from making holes in the metal.

Make sure anything to be fused has a good contact with the parent metal. File flats on to round wires.

The parent sheet requires more heat, so start from the outside, keeping the flame off the small pieces on the surface.

Take care not to overheat the parent sheet. Once the silver has passed the red-hot stage and the surface starts to look shiny, play the flame all over the surface, drawing the shiny look across. If the edges or surface of the base sheet start to distort, remove the flame.

After fusing, air cool before quenching, pickling and cleaning. Fusing causes the surface of the metal to become more porous, so clean well with liquid soap, pumice and a brass brush.

Fusing causes the metal to become hard and brittle. Anneal it to alleviate this.

MARRIED METALS TUTORIAL
Keum-Boo

YOU WILL NEED

- Silver sheet
- 23.5-carat gold foil
- Scalpel or scissors
- Ruler
- Rubber cutting mat
- Small paintbrush
- Water
- Electric hotplate
- Thick sheet of steel or brass
- Curved burnisher
- Pickling solution
- Pumice powder
- Bicarbonate of soda

THE PROCESS

1. Depletion gild the silver to create a fine silver surface.

2. Clean the surface of the silver with a brass brush and pumice powder, followed by bicarbonate of soda to neutralise any pickle, and then hot soapy water to degrease the surface.

3. Place small pieces of 23.5-carat gold foil between two sheets of tracing paper and then cut them on a cutting mat using a scalpel and ruler.

4. Use a small damp paintbrush to pick up the cut pieces of foil and place them on the silver sheet. Lightly brush over the foil so that it makes contact with the silver sheet. This will also remove any air bubbles.

5. Place a thick sheet of steel on an electric hotplate (this helps to diffuse the heat, especially for small items). Place the silver sheet on the steel and turn the hotplate to a medium–high temperature.

6. The silver needs to reach annealing temperature for the gold foil to bond to its surface. A pale pink colour showing through the white of the fine silver surface indicates when the annealing temperature has been attained. Steady the silver with a scriber and use a curved burnisher to gently burnish each piece of gold foil from the centre outwards until it bonds to the silver. Any areas that do not bond should be burnished again.

7. Allow the piece to cool and examine the gold foil to make sure that each piece has bonded properly to the silver. Then pickle, rinse and carefully finish the piece with some fine emery paper.

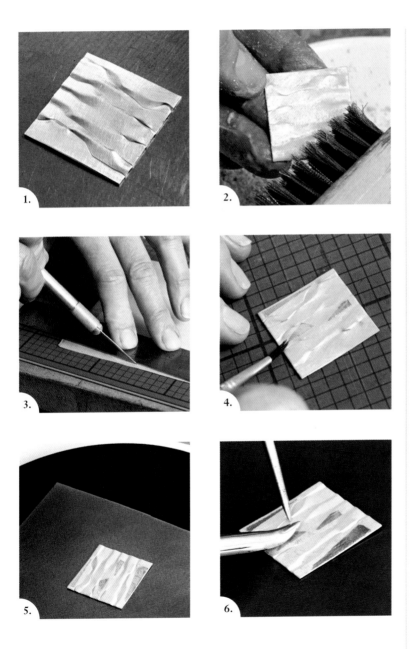

1.

2.

3.

4.

5.

6.

HINTS & TIPS

Complete any fabricating and soldering before applying the gold foil. Heating and soldering after applying the foil may result in the gold fading as it diffuses into the silver, especially if the foil is too thin. Stone setting, cold connections and oxidising can be carried out afterwards.

You can make your own gold foil by placing thin gold sheet between two sheets of paper and passing this sandwich through the rolling mill until it is as thin as it will go. Additional pressure can be applied by placing the gold sheet between two pieces of metal. Anneal the gold regularly by placing a sheet of steel or brass on an electric hotplate. Place the gold sheet on this and heat the steel/brass sheet until the gold is red/annealed. The gold foil should ideally be about 0.0025mm (0.001in) thick.

If there are any pieces or areas of foil that have not bonded to the silver sheet, the process can be repeated.

Use a pin to prick any air bubbles that appear, then burnish the foil down again.

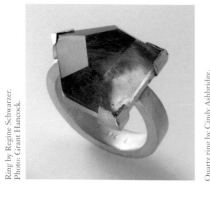

STONE SETTING

Early jewellery was made using natural materials such as animal teeth, bones, shells, stone and wood. After the discovery of gemstones, jewellery became a symbol of wealth and status. Stones are often used symbolically, and some are thought to hold special qualities, such as the ability to heal and protect.

Using stones in a piece of jewellery creates a focal point or feature to a piece and introduces colour and light. Gemstones fall into two groups: precious and non-precious. Precious stones, so-called for their rarity, beauty and hardness, include diamond, ruby, sapphire and emerald, with the rest falling into the non-precious category.

TYPES OF GEMSTONES

Mineral Gemstones: Natural gemstones are mineral crystals formed underground through centuries of heat and pressure. They fall into mineral groups where each different group can contain one or many stones. The most common mineral group is quartz, which has 19 different stones.

Organic Gemstones: Organic materials such as amber, coral, jet and pearl are often used as gemstones in jewellery. These tend to be fairly soft or brittle, making some of them suitable for carving.

Synthetic and Artificial Gemstones: These are manufactured to imitate the look and colour of real gemstones, for example, cubic zirconia is a synthetic diamond. Laboratory-created gemstones have the same chemical and physical characteristics as naturally-occurring stones, but they can have more intense colours and are cheaper to purchase.

Necklace by Terri Logan. Photo: Jerry Anthony.

EVALUATING GEMSTONES

Gemstones are valued for their hardness, colour, clarity and lustre, as well as by their extent of perfection, durability, weight, size and availability. It is important to understand something of these characteristics and of the terms used by gemologists before buying and using gemstones. This will help answer the following questions: is the stone suitable for the piece of jewellery? Will the stone be hard enough for daily wear and tear and able to withstand the setting process? What type of setting does it need?

Hardness: It is important to know the hardness of a stone before working with it. The Mohs scale of mineral hardness is used to identify the scratch resistance of gemstones. Created in 1812 by Friedrich Mohs, it works on the idea of the ability of one material to scratch another. On the Mohs scale, diamond is the hardest at 10 and talc is the softest at 1. Some of the most popular stones are listed on the following page, together with the number that relates to their hardness according to this scale.

Colour: There is a vast range of variation in the colour of gemstones and it is common to find the same stone in several different colours. In addition to this, gemstones are often heat-treated to improve or enhance their colour. The range of variation in colour includes the depth of colour (whether it is pale, dark, deep, etc.), the colour distribution within the stone, and the shade of colour.

COMMON GEMSTONES AND THEIR HARDNESS ON THE MOHS SCALE

 Diamond 10

 Ruby 9

 Sapphire 9

 Emerald 8

 Topaz 8

 Aquamarine 7.5–8

 Tourmaline 7–7.5

 Amethyst 7

 Carnelian 7

 Onyx 7

 Quartz 7

 Peridot 7

 Citrine 7

 Lemon quartz 7

 Rutilated quartz 7

 Garnet 6.5–7

 Tiger's eye 6.5–7

 Moonstone 6–6.5

 Fire opal 6

 Opal 5.5–6.5

 Lapis 5–6

 Turquoise 5–6

 Hematite 5.5–6

 Pearl 2.5–4

 Amber 2–2.5

Clarity: This refers to the transparency of a gemstone, whether or not it has any internal flaws and the pureness of its colour.

Lustre: This describes the quality of the polished surface. Some stones do not polish well, making them less valuable. As a general rule, the harder the stone, the higher the polish.

Inclusions: These are natural flaws within a stone that appear as cracks and fractures. Some stones, such as rutilated quartz, are valued for their interesting inclusions, but in other stones inclusions lower the value. A stone needs to be able to endure the setting process, but inclusions can increase the fragility of a stone. Examine stones carefully for flaws before deciding to use them.

Cut: This describes the style – cabochon or faceted – and the shape – round, oval, square, pear, etc. – of a stone. Cabochons are opaque or translucent gemstones with polished, smooth, rounded tops and flat bottoms. They are also available with a flat top (buff top) and as a double-dome. Faceted stones are transparent gemstones that have small polished flat areas cut at regular intervals and exact angles to reflect and refract light from within the stone and so enhance its beauty.

The figures below illustrate the different types of cuts.

Carat: This refers to the weight of a stone. There are 100 points in a carat. To find the carat weight of a stone, weigh it in grams and then multiply the weight by five.

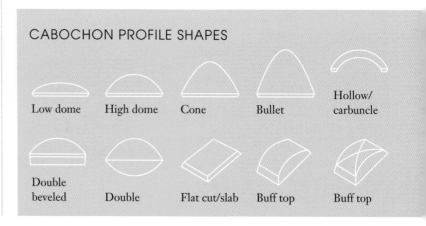

CABOCHON PROFILE SHAPES

Low dome   High dome   Cone   Bullet   Hollow/carbuncle

Double beveled   Double   Flat cut/slab   Buff top   Buff top

TYPES OF SETTINGS

A setting should present a stone at its best, protect it and hold it securely. Some stones determine the type of setting to be used, but it is not always necessary to keep to traditional methods as long as the stone is protected and secure.

Bezel: A thin strip of metal that fits around the stone like a wall. The top edge of the wall is rubbed or pressed over the stone to secure it. Bezels can be made from sheet, purpose-made bezel strip, decorative gallery wire and tube. The back of the bezel can be open or closed according to the stone and the design of the piece. Cabochon and faceted stones can both be bezel set.

Collet: A cone-shaped setting used to set faceted stones. It is usually fabricated from sheet or tube using a collet block and punches. Piercing shapes from the collet will create areas for light to enter and enhance the stone.

Claw: A series of metal prongs that have their ends or claws pushed over the stone. There are several ways to produce a claw setting, including

wires that are bent into a basket-like shape, prongs made from wire or cut from sheet metal and soldered to a bezel or collet and prongs pierced and filed from a collet. The open structure of claw settings allows maximum light to enter, which makes them particularly suitable for use with faceted stones, but they can also be used to set cabochons. This type of setting is very adaptable because it can be used with both regular- and irregular-shaped stones of all sizes.

Gypsy or Flush: A recess made into the surface of thick metal. The stone is set into the recess so it appears to be flush. The metal is pushed over on to the stone like a bezel setting and then burnished. This type of setting works well with curved surfaces and casts rather than fabricated pieces; it is ideal for use with rings. Both faceted and cabochon stones can be gypsy set.

Alternatives: Gemstones can be set in alternative ways by adapting existing setting techniques or using your own creative solutions. It is important that the characteristics of the stone are researched and

considered beforehand and that the stone is secure in its setting. Gemstones with regular shapes and sizes do not have to be used, irregular shapes and sizes can work just as well.

Other types of settings include tension, channel, grain and pavé. However, some of these settings are not suitable for use with silver due to its relative softness compared with gold or platinum. For example, a tension setting relies on the strength of the metal to hold the stone in place, and therefore requires a harder metal than silver.

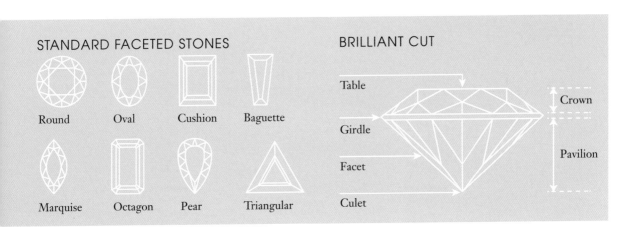

STANDARD FACETED STONES

Round Oval Cushion Baguette

Marquise Octagon Pear Triangular

BRILLIANT CUT

Table

Girdle

Facet

Culet

Crown

Pavilion

STONE SETTING TUTORIAL

Bezel Setting a Stone by Daphne Krinos

YOU WILL NEED

- Silver piece and stone
- 26- or 24-gauge (0.4mm or 0.5mm) fine silver sheet
- 22-gauge (0.6mm) sterling silver sheet
- Round silver wire
- Tin snips
- Ruler
- Scriber/dividers
- Half-round pliers
- Hand, half-round and escapement files
- Emery paper
- Burnisher
- Hard and medium silver solder
- Soldering equipment
- Pickle
- Mandrel
- Hide mallet
- Beeswax or sticky tack
- Bezel pusher
- Small punch
- Repoussé hammer
- Scraper

THE PROCESS

1. Measure a strip of 26-gauge (0.4mm) fine silver sheet and mark it a little wider and longer than needed and then cut it with tin snips. Using half-round pliers, form the strip to make a bezel for the stone to fit into.

2. After soldering the join with hard silver solder, tap the bezel into shape on a mandrel, making sure that the stone is a good fit.

3. Sand the bezel on emery paper to the correct height and to flatten both edges. Solder it to a flat piece of 22-gauge (0.6mm) sterling silver sheet with hard silver solder.

4. Cut the excess silver from the base sheet of the bezel with tin snips and then file and paper it.

5. Solder the completed bezel to the piece using medium silver solder. Paper and finish the piece so that there will be very little or no finishing once the stone has been set.

6. Use a scraper to remove the burr on the inside of the bezel, which was created by sanding or filing. Place a round wire ledge inside the setting to raise the stone up from the base a little. Do not solder this ledge in place, but make it a tight fit.

7. Place the stone in the setting to check that the height of the inner ring is sufficient. Replace or adjust the inner ring as necessary.

8. Support the piece and use a bezel pusher to apply pressure to the bezel and push the silver over to hold the stone at four opposing points.

9. Transfer the piece to a vice, where the setting of the stone is completed using a small punch and hammer to carefully tap the remainder of the silver over on to the stone, working at opposing sides until all the metal is pushed over and the stone is secured.

10. Finish the bezel using an escapement file and burnisher. Carry out any cleaning and polishing of the bezel wall very carefully so that the stone is not damaged.

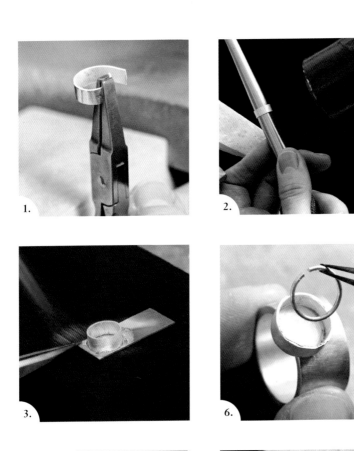

1.

2.

3.

6.

8.

10.

HINTS & TIPS

To work out the length of silver needed to make a bezel, wrap paper around the stone and mark it. Add on a little extra to allow for the thickness of the silver sheet. For round stones multiply the diameter of the stone by 3.5, this will give you the circumference length. For oval stones, add the length to the width, divide by 2 and then multiply by 3.5. Always add on a little extra.

The taller the stone, the higher the bezel needs to be. If the bezel wall is too high, then too much of the stone will be covered and the bezel may pucker during setting.

If the stone does not fit, stretch the bezel on a mandrel with a mallet – never force the stone in. If the bezel is too large, cut it open, remove some metal and resolder.

The setting process can be completed using just the bezel pusher and then a burnisher. If a thicker gauge material has been used for the bezel, use a small punch and hammer to tap the material over.

STONE SETTING TUTORIAL

Claw Setting by Daphne Krinos

YOU WILL NEED

- Stone
- Rectangular sterling silver wire
- 20-gauge (0.8mm) sterling silver sheet
- Sterling silver tube for pendant bail
- Chain and clasp
- Piercing saw and blades
- Scriber
- Hand file
- Half-round ring file
- Flat-nose pliers
- Emery paper
- Hard and medium silver solder
- Pickle
- Mandrel
- Steel block
- Mallet
- Oxidising solution
- Synthetic bristled paintbrush
- Piece of leather

THE PROCESS

1. Make a ring from rectangular silver wire approximately 5mm (¹³⁄₆₄in) larger in diameter than the stone. Solder this with hard silver solder. After pickling, tap it into shape on a mandrel using a mallet, tap it flat on a steel block, then file and paper it.

2. Pierce the material for the claws from 14-gauge (0.8mm) silver sheet. Make sure that the claws will be long enough to hold the stone in position. It is best to cut them too long at this stage.

3. Locate the solder join on the ring and mark the ring for the positioning of the claws, making sure that the solder join is not at one of these points. Place the ring on a charcoal block and hold it with reverse-action tweezers. Solder the strips for the claws on individually at the marked positions using hard and medium silver solder. Quench and pickle the piece.

4. Make any necessary fittings at this stage, such as a pendant bail or brooch pin and hinge, and solder them into position using medium silver solder. Cut and file the claws to the desired length and shape and paper them. Using snipe-nose pliers, bend the claws on the reverse side of the setting into position and bend the claws on the front part of the way over, checking that the stone can still be easily inserted.

5. Remove any marks made with the pliers by papering. Give the piece its final finish. Any oxidising should be done at this stage.

6. Set the stone with flat-nose pliers using a piece of leather to protect the stone and claws. Press each claw down against the stone until it is secured.

7. Give each claw a final squeeze to secure the stone in position using flat-nose pliers without the leather. If oxidising was done and any claws need reoxidising, they should be carefully rubbed with a synthetic bristled paintbrush that has been dampened with Platinol.

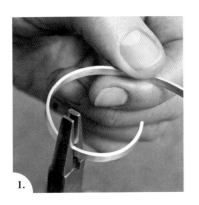

1.

2.

3.

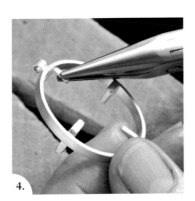

4.

6.

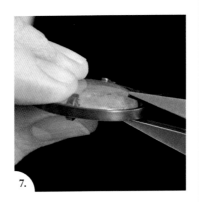

7.

HINTS & TIPS

Use a heavier gauge material when making a claw setting in silver. Additional strength and security can be achieved by soldering claws into drilled holes.

Prongs should be long enough to form the claws and hold the stone safely, but if they're too long they will obscure the stone.

Heat from soldering may weaken claws. If the design allows, work harden the prongs by tapping them with a flat-faced polished hammer against a steel block.

The tips of the claws may need to be filed a little thinner to allow the metal to be pushed over. Always file material from the outside of the claw. Prepare and clean up the claws before setting and burnish them after the stone is secured.

Specialist claw-setting pliers are available but flat-nose pliers can also be used. They should be protected with tape or leather so they do not damage the stone.

STONE SETTING TUTORIAL

Collet Setting a Faceted Stone *by Daphne Krinos*

YOU WILL NEED

- Faceted stone
- 20-gauge (0.8mm) fine and sterling silver sheet
- Sliding calipers
- Piercing saw and blades
- Compasses
- Ruler
- Pencil and paper
- Dividers
- Scriber
- Hand file
- Half-round and escapement files
- Emery paper
- Bezel pusher
- Burnisher
- Hard and medium silver solder
- Pickle
- Collet block and punches
- Hammer
- Graver
- Pendant drill and ball burr
- Clamp
- Beeswax or sticky tack

THE PROCESS

1. Create a collet template by following this sequence:
   - Draw a side view of the stone by measuring the diameter of the stone across the girdle and the height of the stone from the table to the culet. (See the shaded cone in the diagram.)
   - Increase the height a little and draw a line (A–B) parallel with the top of the stone. Draw another line, starting at the centre of A–B and extending down through the point of the cone (C).
   - Draw a parallel line below the point of the stone (D–E) to mark the finished height of the cone.
   - Add sloping lines from both A and B, finishing at C.
   - Set a compass at the radius A–C and draw an arc.
   - Set the compass at radius D–C and draw a second arc.
   - Multiply the width of the stone (A–B) by 3.14 and measure this along the arc from A and mark it at F.
   - Join C with F, creating the template for the cone.

2. Apply the template to the 20-gauge (0.8mm) fine silver sheet and pierce the shape out. After annealing, form the cone using half-round pliers. Make the join to fit well and solder it with hard silver solder, then file and clean it.

3. True the collet using a collet block and punch.

4. File and sand the collet to flatten both edges and clean up the inside. Then solder it to a flat piece of 20-gauge (0.8mm) sterling silver sheet with hard silver solder. After pickling, cut and file away the excess sheet and finish the collet with emery paper.

5. Solder the collet to the piece. Give the piece and the collet a final finish with emery paper.

6. Use a graver to create the seat inside the collet for the stone to sit on. The girdle of the stone should sit just below the top edge of the collet.

7. Place the stone in the collet and set it using a burnisher to massage and push the material over on to the stone, firstly securing it at four opposing points, and then gradually working round to complete the setting and secure the stone. Carry out any further finishing to the collet carefully so as not to damage the stone.

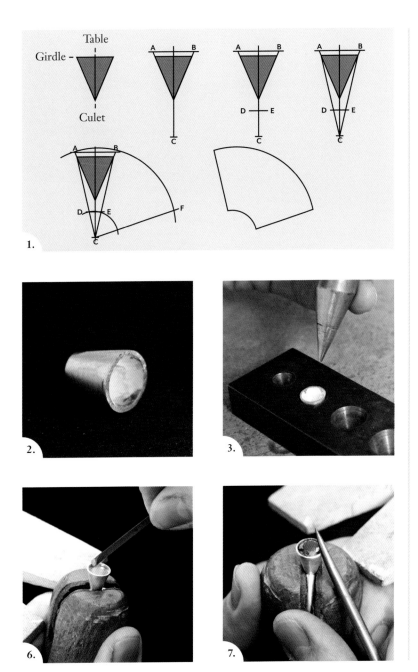

1.

2.

3.

6.

7.

Collets can be fabricated from sheet, or made from tube that has been annealed and then formed in a collet block.

Collets can be open at the back and have pierced areas to allow light to enter and enhance the stone.

Ring shanks can be cut open and the collet soldered between the two cut ends. Any stretching of the ring for re-sizing will distort the collet.

Never heat a silver piece once the stone has been set, as this is likely to damage the stone. If the stone has been heat-treated to enhance its colour, further heat could affect this.

The stone can be set with either a burnisher, a bezel pusher/rocker or a small punch and hammer. Often more than one tool is used to complete the setting before finishing with a burnisher. Setting punches can be made or adapted from old files and punches; they should be hard, not too long, and have small, flat unpolished faces so they do not slip.

Brooch by Julia Rai. Photo: Abby Johnston.

Woven Curtain necklace by Hadar Jacobsen. Photo: Hadar Jacobsen.

Knot bracelet by Hadar Jacobsen. Photo: Hadar Jacobsen.

PRECIOUS METAL CLAY

Precious Metal Clay (PMC) was developed in Japan in the 1990s. It is a combination of organic binders and pure silver particles that have similar working properties to ceramic clay. Simple tools can be used to shape and texture the clay. After drying, the object is heated to a temperature where the silver particles fuse together and the binder burns away, leaving a fine silver piece.

There are endless creative possibilities with this exciting material; a fired metal clay piece can be soldered, filed, polished and worked on like any other piece of silver. Metal clay also lends itself well to texturing and sculptural forms.

TYPES OF METAL CLAY

Precious Metal Clay is available as clay, paste or slip, syringe and paper/sheet. There are two makes of metal clay available: PMC (Original/Standard, PMC+, PMC3) and Art Clay (Art Clay 650 and Art Clay Slow Dry).

METAL CLAY STAGES

It is useful to think in terms of ceramic techniques while working at the clay stage. The fresh clay should be carefully prepared on a clean working area using similar tools to those used for ceramic clay. The metal clay can be cut, textured, shaped and handmade into a multitude of shapes and forms; other materials can be embedded into the clay as long as they can withstand the firing.

Next, the metal clay dries out. There are several stages to this drying-out process as the moisture gradually evaporates from the clay. At the first stage, the surface starts to dry out, but there will still be moisture inside the clay. The clay feels like leather and can still be shaped and formed if this is done with care. At the second stage, the

Necklace by Julia Rai. Photo: Paul Mounsey.

Treasures bracelet by Celie Fago. Photo: Robert Diamante.

surface feels dry, and, while there is still some moisture inside, any forming or shaping at this point would result in the piece breaking. The final stage occurs when all the moisture has evaporated from the clay and it is completely bone-dry. The clay is fragile, but it is possible for very careful sanding to be carried out.

Once it is completely dried out, the metal clay is fired at a temperature close to that of the melting point of fine silver. This firing burns out the binder, which causes the piece to shrink, and sinters the metal particles. The firing should be carried out using a kiln, paying particular attention to firing temperatures and length of firing times. Small items can be fired with a torch.

The fine silver piece can then be worked on like any other piece of silver using silversmithing techniques. Where possible, particular attention should be given to work hardening the piece to strengthen it. Additional parts can be added and the piece re-fired, or any additional parts can be soldered on or attached using other methods, such as cold connections.

PRECIOUS METAL CLAY TUTORIAL

Kiln Firing *by Jessica Rose*

YOU WILL NEED

- PMC3 clay
- Kiln
- Olive oil
- Textured plastic mat
- Plastic roller
- Playing cards or spacers
- Textured wallpaper sample
- Tissue blade
- Clay cutter
- Metal clay paste
- Paintbrush
- Sanding pad
- Needle file
- Brass brush
- Polishing papers
- Hide mallet

THE PROCESS

1. If you are making a ring, measure the finger size and draw this measurement as a line on a piece of paper with 15% added on to allow for shrinkage.

2. Place the clay on a textured plastic mat and roll it into a sausage shape, using a plastic roller with six playing cards stacked on either side to ensure uniform thickness.

3. Remove one playing card from each stack, then place a piece of oiled wallpaper textured side down over the clay and roll it to make an imprint.

4. Cut the clay to the desired size with a tissue blade.

5. Cut shapes from the clay using a mini clay cutter.

6. To apply cutout shapes to the clay piece, paint metal clay paste on to one side of the cutout shape with a brush. Place this on the piece and lightly press it down with one finger for five seconds.

7. After leaving it to dry for 24 hours to evaporate the water in the clay, carefully sand the piece all around its edges using a sanding pad. Use a needle file to clean up inside the cutout shapes.

8. Kiln fire the piece for two hours at a temperature of 900°C (1,650°F)

9. After firing and cooling, brass brush the piece, then rub over it with polishing papers, starting with coarse papers at first, then working down to fine papers.

10. Use your fingers, mandrels and a hide mallet to form the piece.

11. Apply polish as a final finish.

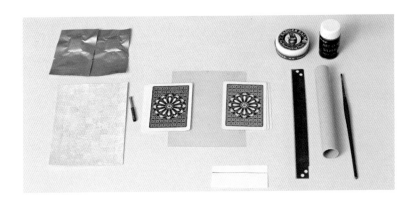

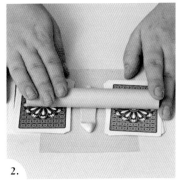

2.

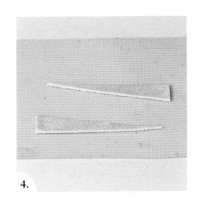

4.

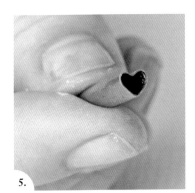

5.

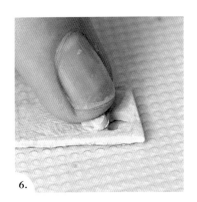

6.

8.

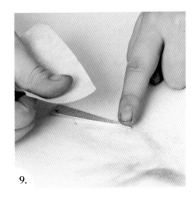

9.

10.

PRECIOUS METAL CLAY TUTORIAL

Torch Firing with a Stone *by Jessica Rose*

YOU WILL NEED

- PMC3 clay
- Torch
- Textured plastic mat
- Plastic roller
- Playing cards or spacers
- Knife
- Heat-resistant stone
- Sanding pad
- Fire brick
- Brass brush
- Polishing papers
- Timer

THE PROCESS

1. Roll out the clay on a textured plastic mat with playing cards stacked on either side to ensure uniform thickness.

2. Use a textured surface to imprint the pattern on to the clay, then cut out the shape using a knife.

3. After applying paste, curl one end over and lightly press it down with one finger for five seconds. Press a heat-resistant stone into the clay.

4. After leaving it to dry for 24 hours to evaporate the water in the clay, carefully sand the piece all around its edges using a sanding pad.

5. Place the piece on a fire brick and torch fire it. Keep the torch moving steadily to distribute the heat evenly. Note the four stages of torch firing:
   a. Smoke
   b. Fire
   c. Black (soot from the clay)
   d. White

6. After the white stage, a peachy glow should be achieved; hold this colour consistently for two and a half minutes to sinter the clay particles.

7. After firing, allow the piece to cool for two to three minutes on the fire brick.

8. Finish the piece with a brass brush and polishing papers – working from coarse to fine papers – then polish it.

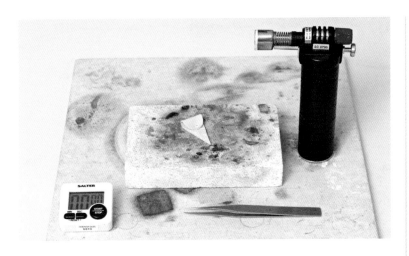

5a.

5b.

5d.

6.

HINTS & TIPS

Stones used in a clay piece must be heat-resistant.

Embedded stones should be pressed down so that the table sits just below the surface of the clay. When the clay shrinks, it will hold the stone in place.

Any material that can withstand the firing temperature can be embedded in the clay, such as fine silver, high-carat gold, stainless steel, brass or copper. To allow for shrinkage, wiggle the embedded piece in the clay to create a space around it.

Metal clay can be quenched to cool after firing, but do not quench if it has a stone or anything else embedded in it.

Turn off any localised lighting before torch firing. This will help you to observe the colour changes at the four stages.

If a flat piece curls at one end during torch firing and does not return to shape, hammer it flat when it has cooled.

Torch firing is not suitable for large pieces.

PRECIOUS METAL CLAY TUTORIAL

Kiln Firing Using the Syringe Technique by Jessica Rose

YOU WILL NEED

- PMC3 syringe metal clay
- Kiln
- Cork clay formers
- Cookie cutter
- Wooden cocktail sticks
- Plasticine
- Paintbrush
- Fire blanket
- Silver eye pin
- Hotplate
- Brass brush
- Barrel polisher
- Polish
- Hide mallet

THE PROCESS

1. Make formers from cork clay. Roll the clay out and cut the shape using a cookie cutter. Insert wooden cocktail sticks at one end.

2. Stick the cocktail sticks into plasticine and leave the cork clay to dry out for two days.

3. Use syringe metal clay to make your piece. Squeeze the syringe gently for as long as possible to release the paste over the cork former, making sure there are lots of connections with the paste.

4. Use a damp paintbrush to dab any areas of paste that are raised. Once fired, these areas of silver can be sharp so using the brush at this stage helps to prevent this from happening.

5. Air dry the piece for a day or two.

6. Once dried, place the piece on a fire blanket and fire it in a kiln at 650°C (1,200°F) for one hour and hold at this temperature for 45 minutes. The cork will burn away.

7. Apply any necessary fittings at this stage, for example for a pair of earrings, insert an eye pin at one end along with some paste. Place the piece on a hotplate to dry out.

8. To complete the application of any fittings, kiln fire the piece at 650°C (1,200°F) for 10 minutes.

9. After cooling, finish the piece with a brass brush, barrel polisher and polish.

1.

3.

4.

5.

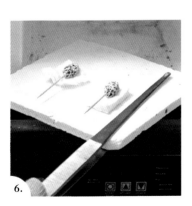

6.

7.

HINTS & TIPS

Keep the tip of the syringe in water to prevent it drying out.

Supports inserted into the cork should be made from a material that that will burn away in the kiln, such as wood.

Speed up the drying process of the cork clay by placing it in an oven at 100°C (212°F).

If barrel polishing a hollow or open form, remember that steel shot from the barrel may become trapped inside. This must be removed.

Once metal clay is exposed to the air it dries quickly, so work swiftly with your piece. Wrap and seal up spare clay straight away so that it can be reused. Pay particular attention to this if you are working in a warm climate. If any spare clay starts to dry out, place it in an airtight plastic box, smear a drop of water inside the lid and then seal the box.

Findings can be integrated by embedding them well into the clay before it dries.

FILIGREE

Filigree is a delicate wirework process that uses fine, twisted wires to create pieces that resemble lace. The name filigree is derived from the Italian words 'filigrana', meaning 'a thread of wire' and 'granum' meaning 'a grain or bead'. Early practice involved the use of wire with small metal granules or balls as ornamentation. While the traditional technique is popular in Indian and Asian metalwork, it has also been reinterpreted in a myriad of ways to bring it up to date, and there are many contemporary examples that develop a modern approach to filigree as a way to express pattern, lightness and complexity.

Filigree work has the advantage of using minimal amounts of metal, which reduces material costs. It is suitable for making lightweight, intricate jewelry and can easily be combined with other techniques, such as stone setting and married metals. However, filigree can be a time-consuming process that requires a lot of patience.

Filigree uses linear designs and involves construction from framed units that contain smaller units of fine, plain or twisted wires. These finer wires are curled into shapes that unite them, creating contacts where they are then soldered to each other, the frame and, sometimes, a ground sheet. Traditionally, the wires do not cross over each other.

TYPES OF FILIGREE

Openwork: Uses wires without a backing. Heavier wires are used for frames in which finer wires are held.

Ground-supported: The wires are soldered to sheet metal.

Combination: Combines openwork and ground-supported filigree.

Enamel/resin: Uses enamel or resin to fill spaces between the wires.

MATERIALS FOR FILIGREE

Sterling or fine silver can be used, but consideration should be given to how strong the piece needs to be. Fine silver is soft and therefore easily manipulated, sterling silver is not as soft but will be stronger. There is a wide range of wires available to choose from – round,

Journey necklace by Yumiko Kakiuchi.
Photo: Byungkwan Cho.

flat, square or rectangular – or, alternatively, wire can be drawn down to suit individual requirements. Traditionally, a frame wire would be 26–20-gauge (0.4mm–0.8mm) with the filler wire 2–4-gauges smaller, so 30–22-gauge (0.25mm–0.6mm). However, there are no hard and fast rules, especially when reinterpreting a technique.

THE FILIGREE PROCESS

There are various stages to work through to achieve a finished filigree piece. The wires must be annealed, then straightened. If twisted wire is to be used, this is made next using the annealed and straightened wires. Flattening then takes place on frame wires and filler wires. The frame wire is then formed and soldered with hard silver solder. Next, the fine filler wires are curled and shaped using any combination of fingers, pliers and jigs. These shapes are then cut and placed in position for soldering. For very fine filigree work, pallions of solder should be avoided: a much neater result, that requires little or no filing or sanding, can be achieved by filing the solder to a dust and sprinkling it on to the fluxed wires or, by sprinkling the solder dust into the flux before applying it to the piece. Pegs, rivets, loops and jump rings can be used to join framed parts or units together. Filigree pieces should never be machine polished as this is dangerous. Pieces should be finished with emery paper, followed by a brass brush. A higher polished finish can be achieved using tripoli and rouge on small polishing mops on a pendant motor, or using polishing threads for hard-to-reach areas.

FILIGREE TUTORIAL

Openwork Filigree by Michael Milloy

YOU WILL NEED

- Square and round sterling silver wire
- Hard and medium silver solder
- Round-nose pliers
- Flat-nose pliers
- Half-round pliers
- Wire cutters
- Piercing saw and blades
- Steel block
- Mandrel
- Hide mallet
- Torch
- Pickle
- Tweezers
- Flux
- Fire brick or charcoal block
- Hand file
- Needle files
- Emery paper
- Brass brush
- Pumice powder
- Pendant motor and polishing attachments
- Polishing compound: tripoli and rouge
- Polishing threads

THE PROCESS

1. Make all the frame wires first. Use round- and flat-nose pliers to bend the wire and form the frames. Prepare the joins by filing.

2. Solder the frame wires on a very flat charcoal block using hard silver solder. After cooling and pickling, clean the join with a file and emery paper, then flatten the fra on a steel block with a mallet.

3. Prepare the finer filler wire by annealing and straightening a length of round wire. Use round-nose pliers to bend the wire into shapes. Cut the shapes from the wire using a piercing saw and file the ends. Where necessary, flatten the shapes on a stee block with a mallet.

4. Place the frame on a very flat fire brick or charcoal block and place all the prepared wires inside, making sure that these make contact with each other and the frame w Flux the joins and place small pallions of medium silver solder on each one (for ver wires, file the solder to a dust and sprinkle on to the fluxed joins). Heat the piece a the solder, making sure that the fine filler wires do not reach the solder flow tempe before the frame wire. Nudge any solder that moves back into position.

5. After cooling and pickling, check the joins and re-solder any that did not solder pr Carry out any cleaning using a needle file and emery paper.

6. Carry out any further forming of the piece using pliers, your hands or mandrels.

7. Finish the piece using a brass brush with pumice powder, and then liquid soap. For polished finish, use tripoli and rouge on small polishing mops on a pendant motor, on polishing threads for hard-to-reach areas.

8. Assemble multiple part pieces using jump rings, pegs, wires or rivets.

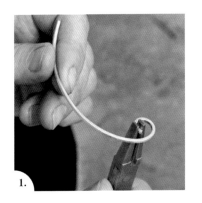

1.

2.

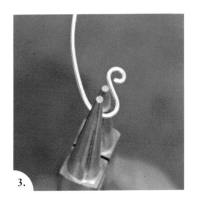

3.

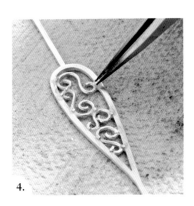

4.

5.

6.

HINTS & TIPS

To ensure shaped filler wires sit level in the frame wire, flatten them against a steel block using a hide mallet and protect round wire by placing a piece of leather or tissue paper on the steel block first.

Filler wires should all be placed in the frame at once and soldered together.

To prevent very fine filler wires moving when the flame is introduced, use a flat charcoal block, place all the filler wires into the frame wire and then place a sheet of metal on top and press it down so that the wires are embedded into the charcoal. This will secure them in their places and prevent them from moving around during heating.

If some joins fracture during shaping, clean the piece and resolder the join, taking care with other nearby joins.

It is important to have good contact between wires that are to be soldered.

Fine wires can be twisted and used as filler wires.

Stacking rings by Ronda Coryell.
Photo: Wesley Clarke.

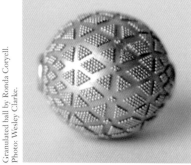

Granulated ball by Ronda Coryell.
Photo: Wesley Clarke.

Ring by Shimara Carlow. Photo: Keith Leighton.

GRANULATION

First used by the ancient Greeks and Etruscans, the granulation technique involves joining tiny balls or grains (traditionally 22/24-carat gold) to a surface for decoration. The grains can be used in a geometric or linear pattern, randomly or minimally to punctuate a design, or to cover areas creating a carpet of texture. The granulation technique can be used to great effect, but perfecting it requires patience and practice.

GRANULATION TECHNIQUES

Proper granulation involves joining tiny balls to a surface so that it is almost impossible to see how they have been attached; they appear to be just sitting on the surface. This is achieved by a fusion-welding technique whereby an alloy of a lower melting point is introduced at the points of contact (this is sometimes described as eutectic bonding). A mixture of copper, organic glue and flux is applied between the two points of contact. When heating, several important stages happen to help achieve the fusion of the granule to the base sheet:

- The copper creates an alloy at the point of contact of the granule and parent sheet and the organic glue carbonises with the heat.
- Both of these lower the melting temperature of the granule and sheet at their points of contact.
- The copper then becomes diffused into the granule and parent sheet, causing them to fuse together without actually melting them.

Earrings by Patricia Tschetter.
Photo: Marilyn O'Hara.

Where granules are touching each other, they also fuse together at their points of contact. To create the lower melting alloy, the granules and the base sheet are copper plated. To achieve this, iron binding wire is placed in a warm pickling solution, together with the granules and sheet. Additional copper pieces can be introduced to the solution, especially if it's new. The copper-plated granules are attached to the base sheet with a mixture of a high-temperature flux and organic glue. Using glue makes this method of granulation ideal for attaching granules to a surface that is not flat.

It is also possible to attach small granules or balls with solder. This method requires careful preparation of the parent sheet by making small depressions or lines for the balls to sit in and using filed solder either sprinkled on to the fluxed granules and parent sheet or mixed with the flux before applying. This method is not as precise and neat as the fusion-welding technique; the solder takes up too much space between and around the granule and base sheet and is visible, making it obvious how the granules have been attached.

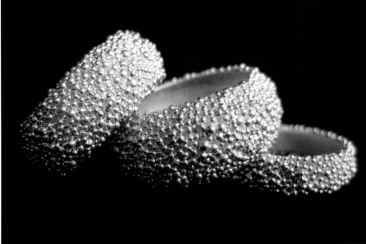

Rings by Linda Lewin.
Photo: Linda Lewin.

Both gold and silver granules can be joined to a silver base. High-carat gold and fine silver granules should be used for the fusion-welding technique, sterling silver granules can be used with the filed solder technique. As well as joining granules to a sheet, they can also be joined granule to wire and granule to granule.

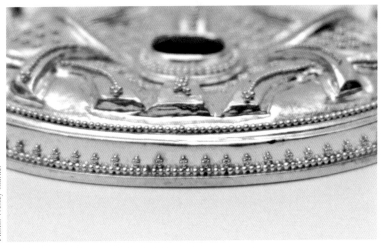

Pendant by Ronda Coryell.
Photo: Wesley Clarke.

GRANULATION TUTORIAL

Making the Granules

YOU WILL NEED

- Charcoal block
- Ball burr and pendant motor
- Jump rings or thin wire in sterling silver/fine silver/ high-carat gold
- Steel tweezers
- Borax
- Torch
- Mesh basket or small glass jar
- Pickling solution

THE PROCESS

1. Make shallow holes in a charcoal block using a ball burr in a pendant motor.

2. Place silver jump rings in a Borax dish to coat them in the prepared flux.

3. Place the fluxed jump rings in the shallow holes of the charcoal block and heat them until they melt. Allow each ball to spin before moving on to the next one.

4. After cooling, place the balls in a mesh basket and pickle them.

5. To prepare granules from wire, place equal-sized lengths of wire in a Borax dish to coat them in the prepared flux.

6. Place the fluxed wires in the shallow holes of the charcoal block and heat them until they melt. Allow each ball to spin before moving on to the next one.

7. After cooling, place the balls in a mesh basket and pickle them, as in Step 4.

1.

2.

3.

4.

5.

6.

HINTS & TIPS

Use a drill bit as an alternative to using a burr in a pendant motor to make a shallow hole in a charcoal block.

The only accurate way to achieve granules of the same size is to use jump rings. Vary the size of jump ring to obtain smaller or larger granules as required.

Use a small glass jar to place the granules in and lower into the pickling tank. This stops the granules from getting lost in the bottom of the tank.

Make lots of granules at once and separate the different-sized granules in bags.

GRANULATION TUTORIAL

Fusion-Welding Granulation

YOU WILL NEED

- Prepared fine silver/gold granules
- Fine or sterling silver sheet
- Iron binding wire
- Small pieces of copper
- Three small glass jars
- Pickling solution
- Mesh basket or small glass jar
- Organic glue (gum arabic or gum tragacanth)
- Auflux soldering fluid
- Small paintbrush
- Charcoal block
- Soldering probe
- Tweezers
- Torch
- Pumice powder
- Brass brush
- Toothbrush

THE PROCESS

1. To build up a layer of copper on the granules, part fill a glass jar with warm pickling solution. Place small pieces of copper and iron binding wire in the solution, along with the fine silver granules.

2. To build up a layer of copper on the parent sheet, clean the silver with pumice powder and a brass brush, then wrap it with iron binding wire and place it in the pickling solution.

3. Mix gum arabic crystals with water in a glass jar, then mix together equal quantities of auflux and gum arabic in a separate jar.

4. Once the granules and sheet start to look pink, remove them from the solution, then rinse and dry them. Using tweezers, dip each individual granule in the organic glue and flux mixture and then place them on the parent sheet.

5. Build up the pattern using the granules.

6. Place the piece under a light to speed up the drying process.

7. When the glue has dried and the granules are secure, gently heat the piece. The organic glue will carbonise (indicated by the black) and burn away.

8. Continue heating the piece past annealing temperature to fusing temperature, this will be indicated by a flash across the surface of the metal and around the granules at their points of contact with the base sheet. At this point, quickly remove the flame.

9. Allow the piece to air cool and then place it in a mesh basket in the pickling solution. The basket stops any granules that have not fused properly to the base sheet from falling to the bottom of the pickle tank. Clean the piece with a toothbrush and pumice powder and examine the granules carefully to make sure they have fused to the sheet.

GRANULATION TUTORIAL
Solder Method

YOU WILL NEED

- Prepared sterling silver granules
- Sterling silver sheet
- Hard silver solder
- Borax
- Rough hand file
- Scribe
- Small drill bit
- Pin vice
- Pickling solution
- Mesh basket or small glass jar
- Charcoal block
- Soldering probe
- Tweezers
- Torch
- Pumice powder
- Brass brush
- Toothbrush
- Emery paper

THE PROCESS

1. Create curved grooves in the silver sheet for the granules to sit in by annealing it three times then passing it through the rolling mill, along with some binding wire. Clean the sheet with a brass brush and pumice powder. Make small sterling silver granules from jump rings.

2. Use a scribe to deepen and define the curved lines created in the silver sheet. File the hard silver solder over a piece of paper using a rough file.

3. Make the Borax into a creamy paste and mix in the filed solder. Carefully paint this paste into the groove on the silver sheet.

4. Place the granules in the Borax dish so that they sit in the paste.

5. Using tweezers, place each individual granule along the grooved line so that they make contact with each other.

6. Introduce a soft, gentle flame to minimise the movement of the flux and granules. Once the flux has settled, nudge any granules that have moved back into place using a soldering probe. Increase the heat, concentrating on the parent sheet. As soon as you see the solder run, remove the flame.

7. Allow the piece to cool, then place it in a mesh basket in the pickling solution. Clean the piece with a toothbrush and pumice powder.

8. Examine the granules carefully to see if each had sufficient solder to attach it to the parent metal. Repeat the soldering process. Carefully paint a small amount of the solder and Borax paste along the line of granules.

9. To avoid solder running on to the parent metal and having to be cleaned up afterwards, remove any excess paste with a piece of paper towel. Run the solder, then cool, pickle and clean the piece with a toothbrush and pumice powder.

10. Clean the immediate area around the granules with emery paper, working through the grades as necessary.

11. Give the piece a final clean with hot soapy water and a small brass brush.

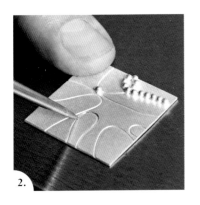

2.

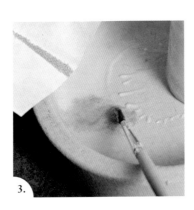

3.

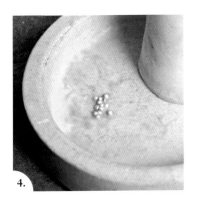

4.

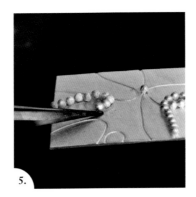

5.

6.

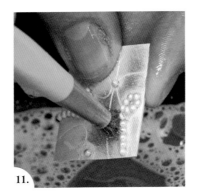

11.

HINTS & TIPS

Always make a depression in the parent metal for the granules to sit in. Do this with a drill bit, a ball burr in a pendant motor, or with the smallest doming punch, create lines or grooves by roller printing or with an engraver.

Always clean the metal with pumice powder and a brush before applying the flux and granules and also before repeated soldering.

It is best to use small amounts of the solder and flux paste and keep repeating the process until the granules have sufficient solder to join them to the parent metal.

Where the granules are in contact with each other, the solder will usually run here too.

Instead of mixing the filed solder with the Borax, try painting the Borax on to the piece, and then sprinkling the solder over the granules with your fingers.

Cynthia Eid's hammered metalwork has won awards for creativity and design, has been featured in many publications and exhibited extensively. Her sculptural jewellery and hollowware is primarily made in Argentium silver and formed through the creative use of hammers and/or a hydraulic press. Cynthia is based in Massachusetts, and teaches regular classes, workshops and short courses. She earned her Master of Fine Arts in Metalsmithing and Jewelry Design from Indiana University in 1980 and has a B.S. in Art Education.

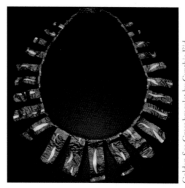

Cynthia Eid

Where do you find your inspiration and ideas?

I love the way that metal can seem so hard, and yet it can be moved and formed as if it were clay. In fact, when I teach forging and forming metal, I help students understand how to move the metal with a hammer by having them think about how a rolling pin can move clay or dough. I love the paradox that 'soft', fluid-looking metal has evolved from flat, stiff rectangles of metal – it's fascinating that a piece can look soft and squishy, but feel hard and unmovable.

I love being able to manipulate metal – making a single complex form out of one piece of metal. I like to make forms that look like something nature could have made, yet are not a copy of something in nature. I prefer inventing new forms, rather than faithfully duplicating one of nature's designs.

Why do you work with the married metals technique?

By using different metals together, I can have colour in my work, without adding gems. If you use gems, they often become the focus of the piece, rather than the metalwork.

Why do you choose to marry non-precious metals with silver?

Working with gold and silver can be very expensive and so I tend to be more conservative and careful in both design and fabrication when working with such precious materials. Copper and bronze also give beautiful colours and patinas with silver, at far less cost. When working with less expensive materials, I feel more free to experiment and to work larger.

Regine Schwarzer was born in 1961 in Hanau, Germany. She grew up in Bavaria and trained in jewellery making and metalwork at the Zeichenakademie Hanau, one of the oldest training institutions in Europe. In 1993 she moved to Australia where she now lives and works in the Adelaide Hills. In 2010 Schwarzer completed a Masters Degree in Visual Arts and Design. Her work is exhibited widely nationally and internationally, is included in many private collections and has been published in several books.

Reflections aquamarine ring by Regine Schwarzer.
Photo: Grant Hancock.

Regine Schwarzer

Where do you find inspiration?

My first encounter with fossils was as a child in the Frankenjura, Germany, digging in the fields with my father, who was a 'fossicker' and collector of rocks and minerals. I rediscovered my passion for finding treasures while travelling through the Australian outback. Inspired by the colours and structures of these minerals, I learned how to shape them and now use them frequently in my work. Working with the material evokes a sense of discovery for me. In search of formations, hidden treasures and patterns reminiscent of landscapes, the stones are sliced open and examined.

Is the design of a piece led by the stone or do you design the piece and then search for the right stone?

It is a selection and design process from the beginning. I explore the diversity of shapes in coloured gems, and I cut them in new, experimental ways. I studied traditional gem cutting techniques, and with that skill as a base, I explore the possibilities and varieties of shapes and colours that translucent and semi-translucent stones have to offer. Traditionally the placement of facets at definite angles on a piece of translucent gem material enhances the reflections and colour flashes that cause scintillation. I have a particular interest in working with inclusions within the stones that conventional techniques discard. These inclusions, or natural impurities, are incorporated into the design of the piece. My intention is to reduce and change the angles on the stones so that their inner life is revealed.

Combinations of materials are selected, tangible structures opposing internal lines and formations, colours harmonising with each other. Visual uniqueness gives value to common materials that are often overlooked or disregarded. By slicing into the materials I discover structures, patterns and colours, traces of their geological history hidden in the layers. The stone is always the starting point for every piece of jewellery I make.

What are the processes that you go through when making a piece?

I like to work with the shape, colour and inclusions of each stone and form them into shapes that go beyond the well-known rounds, ovals and squares. I like to work from the outside to the inside of rough gem material, responding to its random qualities and colour. Cutting a stone is like unveiling the unpredictable and embracing the unexpected.

Kate McKinnon is an author, metalsmith and bead artist who lives and works in her home town of Tucson, Arizona. She has published five books and dozens of magazine articles, and also teaches and lectures internationally. Kate's work in fine silver metal clay won her the coveted Saul Bell Design award in 2005. Her work is focused on connection and structure, and the fun of moving parts.

Kate McKinnon

Where do you find your inspiration and ideas?

From the shapes, forms and textures of the natural world; I love trees and rocks. I'm also inspired by fabulous bridges and buildings, such as the Golden Gate Bridge in San Francisco, the Sydney Opera House and Marina City in Chicago.

Why do you work with metal clay and how did you start using it?

I only work with fine silver metal clay; the finished product is easy to understand from a metalsmithing standpoint, and I can fuse and forge it, just like any type of pure fine silver.

I began using it because I wanted to make innovative findings and clasps for my handsewn beadwork, and it was something I could do without a metalsmithing studio. Or so I thought. As I went further into it,

I realised that metalsmithing skills had to combine with ceramics skills, and that I needed some tools and equipment. I began learning traditional metalsmithing, and never looked back. I love what metal clay can do, but it's not enough for a full metal repertoire.

There are several different ways to work in metal clay, which methods do you use and why?

I have always worked with metal clay with the idea that the work is separated into three parts: ceramics technique (always compressing, not stretching, knowing what to do wet and dry and everywhere in between, and not using slip to glue things together), proper firing and then metalsmithing. If the finished pieces aren't properly constructed, fired and work hardened, then they haven't achieved their full potential.

Tell me about the making of a piece – what are the processes that you go through?

I don't usually start with a drawing of a finished piece. I consider myself a maker of components and small parts. My fascination is with the way things move and connect, and I simply start putting things together in various ways until something sings out at me.

I might make several iterations of a thing before I'm satisfied, and of course there are some themes and forms I've been making forever and will never tire of exploring.

Armenian-born Stepan Terteryan studied jewellery design and manufacture at university in Yerevan. Since settling in the UK, he has established a studio at the Cockpit Arts craft and design centre in London, where he designs and makes limited-edition pieces for retail, along with private commissions. Stepan strives for design that is innovative in concept, yet sustainable in style, and aims for striking pieces that remain comfortable to wear.

Round-hinged silver filigree bracelet by Stepan Terteryan. Photo: John Bellars.

Stepan Terteryan

Why do you work with filigree? Were you commissioned to make a piece or was it a conscious decision to work with this technique?

It was a conscious decision to train in this technique, which is traditional and prestigious in Armenia and has very strong historical foundations. The technical challenge of the metal work appealed to me – the 'engineering' aspect which is required when building a piece of jewellery with filigree.

Traditionally there are several different types of filigree work, do you use a specific type?

The filigree I make uses double-spun fine wires (silver or gold), mounted in a frame and, where possible, unsupported by a backing sheet. I continue to work using 'old-fashioned' foot bellows, which I am now also obliged to make myself! This allows me much more control over the temperature and the force of the flame when soldering than I would achieve using a gas torch.

Filigree can be a time-consuming technique that requires great patience. What are the processes that you go through to make a piece?

The process includes:
- Making my own filigree wire by melting fine and sterling silver together. This creates the necessary combination of softness, tension and spring in the wire.
- Drawing the wire to correct the thickness.
- Spinning two strands of wire together.
- Milling the wire to the correct thickness.
- Each filigree piece will then be shaped, placed, measured and cut to fit the pattern design.
- The solder is prepared by making a bar and filing it to make soldering powder.
- The pieces are then soldered into position.

Open filigree bangle by Stepan Terteryan. Photo: John Bellars.

Patricia Tschetter is an award-winning jewellery designer, whose work has been featured in several magazines and books. She began her jewellery career in 1998 after working as a Marriage & Family Therapist. After taking classes at the Craft Guild of Dallas, she took workshops from various teachers at The Revere Academy in San Francisco, through the Florida Society of Goldsmiths, and others. Her most influential teacher has been Jean Stark, from whom she learned granulation. She lives in Dallas, Texas.

Bee ring by Patricia Tschetter. Photo: Marilyn O'Hara.

Patricia Tschetter

Why do you work with granulation?

After I took my first granulation workshop with Jean Stark, I knew it was the direction for me. It seems to suit my personality. It's ancient history being brought into a modern world. There is so much technology used in jewellery making now, like CAD/CAM, laser welding, etc., [granulation] is one of the last areas that is still done in much the same way it was done 2,000 years ago. It is one of the last places that human hands are still required to touch the

Cuff by Patricia Tschetter. Photo: Marilyn O'Hara.

metal. Yes, granulation can be done with a laser (and larger granules cast), but it doesn't look the same as a hand-granulated piece. As an artist and human, I need that sense of touch.

Traditional granulation is carried out using 22-carat gold and a fusion-welding technique. Tell me about using silver for granulation and your technique.

I use the 22-carat gold granulation technique. I have used fine silver and electrum (silver/gold alloy), which also use the same traditional techniques. However, over the last few years I have used Argentium, which makes granulating with silver so much easier and consistent than either fine silver or electrum. In some ways, it is easier than 22-carat too. With Argentium there is no need for a kiln or dry time before granulation; all I need is a charcoal block, yellow flux and a torch. It is wonderful to work with. I have been able to pierce, granulate, then bend

a ring shank without one granule falling off using Argentium. I could never do that with fine silver, electrum, or 22-carat gold. It is also very versatile as 22-carat can be fused on to Argentium, and vice versa.

What are the processes that you go through when making a piece?

Since I granulate for production work, I can let several pieces rest or dry before firing while I am working on another aspect of a piece or pieces. I am always surprised at how much I can get done when I plan. I listen to music most of the time when I am placing granules. It's sort of meditative for me. Some days I open my studio door to hear the birds. Occasionally, I have to convince a wasp to leave my studio, but even that is sort of meditative for me!

Ute Decker is a leading proponent of ethical jewellery, renowned for her wearable sculptures in recycled silver and bio-resin. She is also one of the first jewellers worldwide to create a collection in fairtrade and fairmined gold. Ute combines organic, angular and clean minimalist dynamic forms with exquisite surface textures, creating striking jewelry art as individual and limited-edition pieces imbued with a refined timeless elegance. Originally from Germany, she is now based in London.

Silk Folds arm sculpture by Ute Decker. Photo: Elke Bock.

Ute Decker

Tell me about the techniques you work with – forging, raising, wire work, texturing. Why do you work with these techniques?

Texture is very important in my work, it gives depth to a piece. I tend to experiment and quite often unexpected textures are the result, which I then refine and allow to evolve. And even though I like the textures that can be achieved by etching, my environmental mind dreads to think what a chemical so potent to etch metal away in minutes will do to our ecosystem.

Land's End arm sculpture by Ute Decker. Photo: Elke Bock.

Thus I avoid toxic chemicals. After all, I am a creative person and feel that I can find many other ways to achieve interesting textures. In our studio, we use non-toxic citric acid for pickle and eggs to oxidise silver – of course only the organic free range eggs from the local farmer's market!

Many of my larger wearable sculptures are created through anti-clastic forging. Beautifully dynamic forms can be achieved through this method and I was very fortunate to attend two five-day workshops given by Benjamin Storch – one of the great masters of the anti-clastic technique.

Tell me about your use of ethical silver for your work.

When first starting out as a studio jeweller, I was horrified to learn about the environmental and social impact of metal mining. It took a long time to find ethical suppliers

and since then I have shared background information, my expertise and links to ethical metal and gemstone supplier on my website: www.utedecker.com.

The quality of 100% recycled silver is equal to conventional silver, the malleability and colour are exactly the same, even the price is the same.

What processes do you go through when making a piece?

My work is to a large extent process driven. While I go through a series of sketches, once in the studio I allow serendipity to play her part in the creation of a piece. I enjoy the creative process and thus prefer to make one-offs or small series in which each piece will be different from the previous.

SECTION TWO
MATERIALS, TOOLS AND RESOURCES

TYPES OF SILVER

FINE SILVER 999

99.9% silver, this is silver in its pure state. It will not oxidise or tarnish, and does not require pickling after heating. Fine silver is soft and has limited use for jewellery making. However, because it is easily worked, it is ideal for using when raising, making rub-over settings for fragile stones and for some wirework, as well as granulation. Fine silver is what results when Precious Metal Clay is fired; additional steps are needed to work harden it after firing to produce pieces strong enough for jewellery.

STERLING SILVER 925

In order to maintain strength, silver is usually alloyed with copper. Sterling silver is an alloy containing 92.5% silver and 7.5% copper; it is standard in many countries and has been since the fourteenth century. With the decrease in silver and the addition of copper, there is an increase in tarnishing and susceptibility to firescale.

BRITANNIA SILVER 958

Britannia silver is less commonly known than sterling silver. It is an alloy of 95.8% silver and 4.2% copper. The greater proportion of silver means it is less susceptible to firescale and is softer than sterling silver, making it easier to work. It also work hardens less quickly. These qualities make it ideal for enamelling, spinning and forming. It was introduced in England by an Act of Parliament in 1697 to replace sterling silver as the standard for silver items and as part of a recoinage scheme by William III.

The intention was to control the practice of clipping and melting sterling silver coins to produce silver articles by maintaining a higher standard for these pieces. It is still used in the UK and Ireland and is denoted by the silver hallmark 958.

ARGENTIUM SILVER

The copper contained in silver alloys oxidises during annealing or soldering applications and this can be seen as a dark stain on the surface of the metal called firescale or firestain. This oxide can penetrate deep into the surface of the silver, forming unsightly stains; it can be extremely difficult and sometimes impossible to remove from finished pieces. This problem is particular to sterling silver. Alloy development remains very active, and recently a number of sterling silver alternatives have been developed, where a small amount of the copper in the alloy is replaced with an element, or combination of elements, that prohibits the formation of firescale. One such alloy is Argentium silver. Invented in 1996 by Peter Johns at Middlesex University in England, Argentium is now produced in the USA and Italy from recycled silver and can be bought in a wide range of products through a number of suppliers worldwide. There are currently four different alloys available: Argentium® Sterling Silver, also known as Argentium® Original, which has 93.5% pure silver, copper and a small amount of germanium replacing some of the 7.5% copper that is usually in sterling silver. Argentium® 960-Pure, a Britannia grade alloy, contains 96% pure silver with copper and germanium. There are also two alloys that were specifically developed for casting applications (Argentium 935 and 960 Pro). With the introduction of germanium, Argentium boasts a firescale-free sterling silver alloy, with excellent tarnish resistance and greater ductility than traditional sterling silver. This means that it can be worked longer and further between each annealing; it is also easily fused and welded, making it ideal for techniques such as granulation. Working with this new sterling is a little different from traditional sterling silver and certain procedures need to be followed to ensure optimum results.

RECYCLED SILVER

Sustainability and recycling are issues that many jewellers are concerned with. 2011 saw the launch of fair trade and fair mined gold and an increasing demand for traceability through fairmined and fairtrade silver. In the meantime, jewellers can find a more sustainable way of using silver by purchasing 100% recycled silver through a small number of suppliers.

SILVER AVAILABILITY AND PRODUCTS

Silver can be bought in a wide range of products from bullion dealers and specialist jewellery material suppliers. The range of products include sheet in various gauges; wire, rod and tube in many different sizes and profile shapes; chain; findings; casting grain; and Precious Metal Clay. The widest range of products can be found in sterling silver.

Silver products are sold by weight and the price, determined by the market value, changes from day to day. Some products, such as tube, are more expensive to buy despite the value of silver, because of additional manufacturing costs producing these items. Scrap silver can be recycled and many bullion dealers offer this service. Scrap silver and bench sweepings should be saved, keeping clean scrap separate, as this can be sold for a higher price.

SILVER FORMATS

1. Square Wire
2. Rectangular Wire
3. Round Wire
4. Triangular Wire
5. Round Rod
6. Square Tube
7. Round Tube
8. Grain
9. Sheet

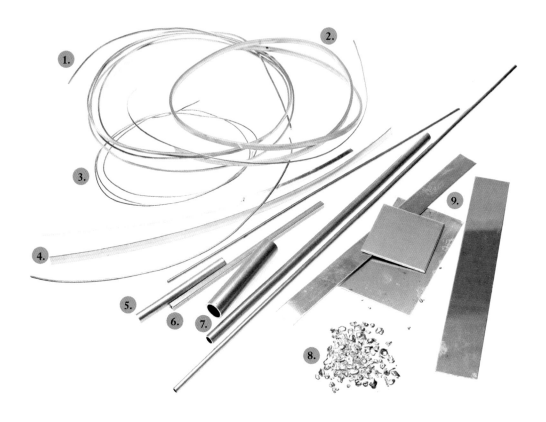

TOOLS

THE WORKBENCH

The Jeweller's Bench and Workshop:

The workbench should be about 95cm (37in) from the floor with a thick, sealed bench top and sturdy legs. It should not wobble, so may need to be secured to the wall. The semi-circular cutout has a bench peg or pin mounted in the centre that is used to support the work and should have a V-shape cut from it. A leather bench skin hangs from the underside of the bench semi-circle and is used to catch metal filings and dust. The flexi shaft/pendant motor is secured to one side of the bench. Good light is important and a suitable work light should be secured towards the back of the bench. The pickling tank must be kept away from tools, either to one side of the bench or in a separate area. Tools such as pliers and hammers should be stored so that they can be easily seen and reached. A bench vice can be secured to the workbench. To ensure that you are working comfortably and at the correct height, an adjustable-height office chair that offers good support is essential.

Leather Bench Skin:

Hangs from the underside of the bench semi-circle and is used to catch metal filings and dust.

Workbench Light:

Clamps or screws on to the jeweller's workbench.

BENCH TOOLS

Flexi Shaft/Pendant Motor:

A motor and long flexible shaft with a handpiece into which various attachments can be secured, such as drill bits and burrs.

Ring Sizer:

For stretching and shrinking rings.

Bench Vice:

For securing tools or articles that are being worked on. Metal, rubber or felt jaw protectors should be used to prevent the serrated jaws marking the silver.

Drawplate:

For straightening, work hardening and reducing the size of wire and altering its profile. Mount in a bench vice.

Draw Tongs:

For use with a drawplate to pull the wire through.

Sandbag:

Made from thick leather and filled with sand, used for supporting work or tools. Techniques carried out using the bag include sinking, doming, raising and engraving.

MACHINERY

Bench Drill:

For drilling holes. Can be used with a drill press vice to securely hold work during drilling.

Hydraulic Press:

For press forming and embossing.

Rolling Mill:

With sheet and wire rollers for reducing the thickness of metal.

Ultrasonic Cleaner:

Uses ultrasonic sound waves to vibrate a heated cleaning solution that lifts away dirt and polish.

Pickling Tank:

Thermostatically heats diluted sulphuric acid or safety pickle in which metal is cleaned after being heated or soldered.

Polishing Motor/Buffing Machine:

Used in conjunction with various mops, wheels and compounds for finishing surfaces.

Barrel Rotary Tumbler/ Barrel Polisher:

Used with steel shot to polish, burnish and work harden. Suitable for metal clay and chains.

HAND DRILLS, DRILL BITS AND BURRS

Wheel Brace/Hand Drill:

For drilling and twisting wire.

Swivel Pin Vice:

For holding small tools such as drills and burrs when drilling by hand or when making fine adjustments to stone settings.

High-Speed Twist Drills:

Made from steel and available in various sizes. Can be used with the bench or hand drill, smaller sizes can be used in a pendant motor.

Steel Burrs:

Various different shapes and sizes are available: cone, cylinder, flame, round, stone setting. Used in the flexi shaft/pendant motor to cut or grind, shape, or give pattern to a surface.

Carborundum Abrasive Burr:

Abrasive made of a hard mineral consisting of aluminium oxide, used in conjunction with the flexi shaft/ pendant motor to remove metal. Various different shapes and sizes are available.

MEASURING

Steel Rule:
Use with a scriber or dividers.

Scales:
For weighing metal and finished pieces. Useful for working out final metal costs when pricing work.

Vernier Caliper/Precision Sliding Caliper:
For taking internal and external measurements.

Lightweight Mandrel:
For measuring rings. Ring sizes are marked along the lines.

Ring Gauges:
For measuring fingers. Each ring is marked with a size.

Adjustable Bangle/Bracelet Gauge:
For measuring hands and wrists.

MARKING

Scriber:
Used freehand or in combination with a steel rule or square to mark out measurements and designs as well as score the surface of the silver.

Dividers:
Used for marking out measurements, circles and parallel lines by scoring.

Steel Square:
Used with a scribe to mark lines, create a square from a non-square piece of sheet and to confirm if a line is at right angles to another.

Centre Punch:
Tapped with a jobbing hammer to make an indent to locate a drill bit when drilling holes.

Decorative and Letter Punch:
Each steel punch has a motif/letter on the end. Struck with a jobbing hammer to make patterns, textures, etc.

CUTTING

Side Cutters:
For cutting hard wire up to 12-gauge (2.0mm).

Tin Snips:
Unsprung straight-bladed shears for cutting solder and thin sheet.

Saw Frame/Jeweller's Saw/ Piercing Saw:
Sprung metal frame and wooden handle, holds a fine blade under tension. Used for cutting, piercing and fretwork.

Saw Blades:
Used in a jeweller's saw for cutting, piercing and fretwork. Available in a range of sizes from 4 (the coarsest) to 8/0 (the finest). The most common size used is 2/0.

Tube Cutter:
For holding tube securely while cutting with a piercing saw. The tube stop can be adjusted to the required length and allows for the same length of tube to be cut many times.

Disc Cutter:
To cut discs or holes in annealed silver sheet up to 21-gauge (0.7mm).

FILING

Hand File, Half-round Ring File:
Available in a range of cuts for removing metal and cleaning up joins inside rings and curves.

Hand File, Flat:
Available in a range of cuts for removing metal and cleaning up joins, both cut 0 and cut 2 are essential.

File Handle:
Provides comfort for hand files.

Needle Files:
Available in a range of cuts, sizes and shapes for removing metal and cleaning up joins on intricate pieces.

Riffler Files:
Have shaped and curved ends available in a medium cut for removing metal on intricate pieces.

Escapement Files:
Fine watchmaker's files, usually cut 6, available in a range of shapes and used in small areas for delicate work.

HAMMERS

Texturing Hammers:
Double-sided hammers for quick and easy texturing.

Chasing Hammer:
The large, flat face is used for tapping chasing punches and the domed end is used for forming rivet heads and texturing silver.

Riveting Hammer:
A lightweight hammer with a small head, ideal for securing rivets, hardening and texturing silver.

Jobbing/Ball-peen Hammer:
A general purpose hammer with the flat face used for hitting tools such as punches, and the domed end used for texturing.

Blocking Hammer:
One deep domed and one shallow domed face, used in the first stages of raising on a soft support such as a sandbag or wooden recess.

Raising Hammer:
Has two rectangular curved faces, one face is curved more than the other. Used in conjunction with a stake to stretch metal for raising and forging. Hammer faces should be kept polished and in good condition.

Planishing Hammer:
Two round faces, one flat and one gently curved. Used in conjunction with a stake to remove marks made by other hammers, to work harden and to subtly texture.

MALLETS

Rawhide Mallet:
Used in conjunction with a metal stake or mandrel for shaping and flattening without marking the silver. Available in several different-sized heads.

Bossing Mallet:
Made from wood and used for the initial stages of doming metal ready for raising.

PLIERS

Parallel Pliers:
Unsprung and useful for holding, folding, bending and removing kinks from wire without damaging the silver.

Snipe-nose Pliers:
Tapered jaws used for bending, chain work and accessing awkward areas.

Flat-nose Pliers:
Two flat-faced jaws used to bend, fold and straighten.

Half-round Pliers/Ring Pliers:
One flat-faced jaw and one half-round jaw used to bend and curve. The half-round jaw curves the metal, while the flat jaw helps reduce marks on the outside of the curve.

Round-nose Pliers:
Used to shape wire and make loops and curves.

STAKES

Bench Anvil:
For shaping, flattening and supporting work. Can be used on the bench or secured in a vice.

Steel Bench Block/Flat Stake:
A general-purpose tool, used with a mallet/hammer to flatten sheet or to act as a hard plate against which a piece of metal may be punched or supported. The surface should be kept clean and polished, as any marks will be transferred to the metal's surface.

Steel Dapping/Doming set:
For creating domes. Various wooden punches are also available.

Swage Block:
Used to form sheet into channels or tube using a doming punch on its side or a steel former. Can also be used to create D-section wire by hammering round wire into the channels.

Silversmithing Stakes:
Used with various hammers for forging, raising and planishing metal.

Three-arm Stake:
Made from steel and clamped securely in a vice, the stake is used with various hammers to form/shape metal. Metal is placed over the appropriate stake and hammered to achieve the shape required.

MANDRELS

Round Bangle Mandrel:
Used to shape bangles or other curved forms with the use of a wooden mallet or hammer. Keep the surface of the mandrel clean as marks will be transferred to the metal.

Round Marked Ring Mandrel/Triblet:
For forming and truing rings on. Ring sizes are marked on. Can be mounted in a bench vice.

Mandrel/Triblet:
To bend, shape and true forms for rings, bezel settings, etc. Available in various different shapes and sizes. Can be mounted in a bench vice.

Wire Wrap Mandrels:
Mandrels to create consistently-sized loops.

HEATING AND SOLDERING

Flux Brush:
To apply flux, paste or liquid.

Borax Cone:
A dry form of flux used with water and a Borax dish to form a paste that is then used as a flux to keep the join area clean while soldering.

Borax Dish:
Unglazed ceramic dish used with a Borax cone and water to create a flux paste.

Auflux/Auroflux:
A liquid flux that is primarily used for gold but can also be used for silver.

Steel Tweezers:
For picking up work during and after heating and for picking up pieces of solder.

Reverse-action Tweezers:
Has one straight and one curved tip. The tweezers are sprung to allow the handles to be squeezed to open the arms. Useful for helping to support pieces when soldering. Has insulated hand grips.

Third Hand Base:
An all-angle stand to hold reverse-action tweezers. Used to help support pieces during the soldering process.

Brass Tweezers and Tongs:
Used for depositing and removing articles from the pickle solution or holding material when hot.

Plastic Tweezers:
Used for removing articles from a pickle solution, and depositing and removing pieces from etching and colouring solutions.

Soldering Pick/Probe:
Used to pick up solder as well as help guide the molten solder along the join.

Binding Wire:
Used for binding and holding parts together during soldering.

Hand Torch:
Butane gas torch suitable for soldering and heating.

Gas Torch:
For annealing, soldering and all other heat applications. Must be connected to bottled propane gas. Kit consists of regulator, hose, handle and a range of different-sized burners.

Heatproof Blocks and Sheets:
Used to solder and anneal on, several should be used together to provide adequate protection for the bench. The block can be broken into shapes to support the item being soldered.

Charcoal Block:
For soldering and melting small amounts of metal. The surface can be carved to embed pieces before soldering. Charcoal under the flame creates a reducing atmosphere for a cleaner soldering environment. Holds the heat well and reflects it back to the work for maximum soldering results. Retain the block shape by wrapping the sides tightly with binding wire before use.

Revolving Stand:
A rotating stand on which a heat-resistant block/sheet is placed on top allowing the work to be turned during heating and soldering. Good for evenly heating a piece as it enables the heat source to be focused from different directions throughout the process.

Rouge Powder:
Mixed with water to form a paste, which can be painted on joins that have already been soldered to prevent the solder from running in subsequent solderings.

Heat Insulating Gel:
Used to protect areas not requiring heat when soldering, such as other solder joins.

METAL CLAY

Spacer and Roller Set:
Spacers are used to create different thicknesses when rolling clay.

Teflon Worksheets:
For working on with metal clay.

Clay Shapers:
For precise, controlled carving and detailed work.

Patterned Brass Sheet:
For texturing metal clay. Various patterns are available.

Cutters:
To cut clean, precise shapes in metal clay.

Wooden Ring Mandrel on Stand:
For modelling metal clay when making rings, etc.

Needle Tool:
Useful for metal clay.

Scalpel:
Useful for cutting metal clay.

Sponge Sanding Pads:
Use dry on dry clay or wet on metal clay after firing. Various grits are available. Soft, flexible and re-usable, they can be cut into smaller pieces or strips with scissors.

Agate Burnisher:
Used instead of a steel burnisher for fired and unfired metal clay, as well as burnishing gold foil to silver for Keum Boo. It will not damage stones and can be used to close bezels.

Gold Foil:
Not restricted to metal clay, this can also be used with sterling and fine silver.

Kiln:
For firing Precious Metal Clay.

ENGRAVING

Graver:
Made from steel and used for engraving a metal surface. Supplied in a longer length than required, which needs to be cut down to suit personal requirements. Various different shapes are available.

Flat Scorper:
Made from steel and used by setters and engravers for cutting and carving into metals.

Engraver's Vice:
An adjustable frame with holes and pegs to hold small pieces for engraving and stone setting.

Eyeglass:
A magnifier held in the socket of the eye and used for engraving and fine work. Different focal lengths are available.

Oilstone:
A double-sided carborundum stone with one medium and one fine side, used with machine oil to sharpen gravers and other tools.

Arkansas Stone:
A fine grade natural stone that polishes as well as sharpens. Used with oil for gravers and other tools.

Spherical- and Balloon-shaped Wooden Handles:
Sit comfortably in the palm of a hand, suitable for use with gravers, scorpers, etc. To fit, the tang of the tool is heated and inserted into the neck of the handle, then tapped down to make it secure.

CHASING AND REPOUSSÉ

Chasing and Repoussé Punches:
10cm (4in) long steel punches ground and filed to shape at one end. A basic set of about 20 should include: tracing, modelling, doming, planishing and matting.

Pitch Bowl and Support:
Cast-iron hemispherical bowl containing jeweller's pitch. The pitch supports the metal during chasing and repoussé. A sandbag or wooden ring provides support for the bowl.

STONE SETTING

Loupe:
A hand-held magnifier used for stone setting and fine work. Different focal lengths are available.

Bezel Roller:
Made from a soft metal to provide slip-free control and to prevent damage. Used to push the metal of a rub-over or bezel setting over a stone.

Pusher:
Made from a soft metal to help provide slip-free control and prevent damage. With a flat square end and a wooden handle, it's used to push the metal of a rub-over or claw setting over a stone.

Burnisher:
For burnishing (polishing) a surface. Useful for hard-to-reach areas, stone setting and removing slips made when engraving. Also available curved. Requires a handle.

Scraper:
A triangular blade for removing metal, useful for bezel settings and removing slips made when engraving.

Collet Plate and Punch:
Used for forming, stretching, reducing or changing the shape of a collet. Available with 17 or 28° angles and in various shapes: round, oval, square, emerald cut, pear, hexagonal and rectangular.

CASTING

Cuttlefish:
For casting, bones are sanded flat and the soft part is either carved or an object is pushed into it.

Carving Tools:
For carving cuttlefish, creating air vents, refining sand-casting moulds.

Aluminium Casting Rings:
For sand casting, the sand is packed into one ring before pushing an object into it to make an impression to cast from. The rings are then joined and sand fills the second one.

Casting Sand/Delft Clay:
A dense and oily reusable sand used for casting. It picks up details from impressions made by objects.

Crucible/Scorifier:
A ceramic vessel for melting small quantities of silver for casting using a torch.

Tongs:
For use with a square crucible/scorifier.

ABRASIVES AND POLISHING

Pumice Powder:
A fine abrasive powder used on a rinsed article (without drying) after pickling, to create a clean degreased surface on which to solder. A pumiced surface can be used as a final finish.

Emery Paper:
Various grades are available. They are used dry for surface finishes after filing. For optimum results, use the papers in sequence from coarsest to finest. Can be cut to the required shape/size.

Abrasive Rubber Block:
Impregnated with an abrasive, can be cut into a required shape or used in block form. Suitable for cleaning or for creating a satin finish. Various grades are available, each denoted by a different colour for easy recognition.

Scotch-Brite and Wire Wool:
For cleaning up and surface finishing. Wire wool is available in various grades from very abrasive to fine.

Split Mandrel/Pin:
Used in a flexi shaft/pendant motor with a strip of abrasive paper threaded through the slot in the pin and wound around tightly, for cleaning up inside rings, etc. As the paper wears, it is cut back.

Rubber Burr:
Impregnated throughout with an abrasive compound, various grades and shapes are available. Used in conjunction with a flexi shaft/pendant motor, for polishing by working down through the grades to obtain the best results.

Radial Abrasive Disc:
Used in conjunction with a flexi shaft/pendant motor for cleaning, pre-polishing and texturing. Ideal for hard-to-reach areas. Available in various grades from coarse to super fine.

Silicon Rubber Wheel:
Impregnated with an abrasive compound, available in coarse to fine grades. Used in conjunction with a flexi shaft/pendant motor for polishing, needs a screw in the top mandrel to mount the wheel. The shank of the mandrel is then secured in the collet/chuck of the pendant motor.

Brass Pendant Wheel:
Used in conjunction with the flexi shaft/pendant motor to give an even, shiny, satin surface finish, or to clean an area prior to soldering. Available as a pendant cup and pendant point. These must be lubricated with liquid soap and water to prevent the brass binding to the surface of the metal.

Scotch-Brite Pendant Wheel:
Used in conjunction with the flexi shaft/pendant motor to give a fine satin surface finish.

Pendant Frosting Wheel/ Flick Mop:
Used in a flexi shaft/pendant motor to create a satin finish on a surface. Available in various grades from coarse to extra fine. Note: eye protection must be worn.

Buffing/Polishing Pendant Wheel:
Used with a polishing compound in conjunction with the flexi shaft/pendant motor to polish small or hard-to-reach areas. Available in wool, calico and felt.

Felt Pendant Wheel:
Used with a polishing compound in conjunction with a flexi shaft/pendant motor to polish small or hard-to-reach areas. A different point should be used for each metal and compound. Various shapes are available.

Scotch-Brite Wheel:
Used in conjunction with a buffing/polishing machine, but without a compound, to give a fine satin surface finish.

Polishing Compounds:
Tripoli is a coarse compound used for the initial polish of silver, after using emery paper, with a medium to hard buffing wheel/mop e.g., calico. Rouge is used for the final polish to obtain a fine mirror finish. Ideal for use with a soft buffing wheel/mop e.g., reflex, chamois, wool or calico.

Buffing/Polishing Mop:
Fits on the spindle of a buffing/polishing machine. A different mop should be used for each metal and compound. Mops should be cleaned before each use with a mop rake because a buildup of compound may harden and leave drag effects on the metal surface. Clean mops by soaking overnight in a solution of hot water, liquid detergent and ammonia.

Polishing Threads:
Use with or without compounds to polish between small areas, such as settings, where the use of a mop is not practical.

Tapered Felt:
For use on the buffing/polishing machine to polish inside rings. A different mop should be used for each metal and compound.

Protecting and Polishing:
Microcrystalline Wax: for protecting and enhancing the colour of oxidised silver. Glanol®: a gentle metal polish with surface protection. Duraglit: silver polish wadding.

Silver Cleaning Cloth:
Impregnated with tarnish remover and used for removing finger marks and tarnish from finished pieces.

Brass Brush:
For cleaning and surface finishes. Use under running water with a detergent to prevent any brass particles becoming embedded in the surface of the metal.

Bench Brush:
A multi-purpose brush that can be used with water and detergent to degrease or to clean polish residue from a polished piece. Can be used with pumice powder to clean silver after pickling or etching.

Glass Brush Pen:
For metal preparation, cleaning the surface of metal, or to produce a matte/brushed finish. Note: use under running water to prevent glass fibres becoming impregnated in the skin. Goggles and gloves should be worn.

Steel Shot:
Used in a barrel polisher with barreling soap to polish, burnish and work harden silver. A mix of shapes is recommended.

CHEMICALS

Solvents and Degreasing:
Lighter fuel, white spirit and acetone are used for dissolving and removing stop-out varnish, adhesives, marker pen, etc. Denatured alcohol/methylated spirit is used for degreasing.

Ultrasonic Cleaning Fluid:
For use in professional ultrasonic cleaners to help remove dirt, polish, grease, tarnish, etc.

Barreling Soap:
A burnishing powder, used with steel shot and water in a barrel tumbling machine to deburr, pre-polish and work harden silver. It also contains a medium that prevents the steel shot from rusting.

Iron III/Ferric Nitrate Salts:
For etching silver. Follow manufacturers' instructions.

Three-In-One Oil:
To lubricate tools and machinery and to prevent rust forming on tools.

Beeswax:
Used as a lubricant on saw blades when piercing metal. Helps to prevent the blade sticking.

Cut Lube:
For the lubrication of steel burrs, piercing blades, drills, etc.

Stop-Out Varnish/Black Polish:
Applied with a brush to conceal areas where the etching process is not required, the liquid should dry before the item is placed in the etching acid. Remove with acetone.

Pickling Powder:
Mixed with water to form a solution that has a sulphuric acid base. Used warm to remove surface oxides and flux from silver after heating and soldering. Avoid contact with skin (it will cause irritation) and clothing (it will cause damage upon contact). When placing objects in and out of solution, always ensure the use of either plastic or brass tongs/tweezers. Always add pickle powder to water. Gives off fumes, so must be used in a well-ventilated area. Follow manufacturer's instructions.

Oxidising Solution/Liver of Sulphur/Ammonium Hydrosulphide:
Used to blacken silver. This concentrated liquid needs to be diluted before use. Always follow manufacturer's instructions. Platinol gives a deep black to pale grey finish. Pour a small amount into a plastic container before either immersing or using a brush to cover the area to be oxidised, then rinse in water. Keep used solution separate, do not add used solution to unused solution. Store in a cool, dark area for prolonged life. Note: fumes are given off from both of these chemicals so they must be used in a well-ventilated area or fume cupboard. Wear protective gloves, goggles and a mask.

Red Masking Lacquer/Lacomit:
Used for blanking out areas where gold plating is not required. It is applied with a brush and removed, after the plating process, with lacquer thinner/lacomit remover. Note: gives off fumes, so must be used in a well-ventilated area. Wear a respirator mask as well as protective gloves.

Lacquer Thinner/ Lacomit Remover:
Used to remove and thin plating resist. Note: gives off fumes, so must be used in a well-ventilated area. Wear a respirator mask as well as protective gloves.

HEALTH AND SAFETY

Most jewellers work in small studios and workshops or from home; wherever the workshop is located, it is vital that certain health and safety procedures are practiced. The workshop should have a first-aid kit, eyewash and a small fire extinguisher. Good ventilation is important, if in doubt work outside, wearing a suitable respirator. Common sense plays a very important role, as well as taking adequate precautions and following some simple safety rules.

MACHINERY

Always read manufacturers' instructions and use machinery correctly. Bench drills and buffing/polishing machines should be secured to the workbench to prevent them from moving around with the vibrations that they create. Install and use machine guards when they are provided and wear safety glasses. Tie back loose clothing and hair. Wear a dust mask when carrying out procedures that create dust, such as buffing/polishing. Never wear gloves when polishing; finger guards may be used where necessary, but these can come off easily if caught in the buffing wheel/polishing mops. If anything becomes snatched or caught in the buffing wheel/polishing mop, let go of it and turn the machine off before attempting to recover it. Chain should never be polished on a buffing/polishing machine because it can be easily snatched away; use a rotary tumbler/barrel polisher instead.

CHEMICALS

Where possible, these should be stored in a lockable metal cupboard. Always read manufacturers' guidelines and obtain health and safety data sheets from the supplier. Chemicals must be clearly labelled and any used or mixed solutions should include the date of preparation. Wear an apron to protect your clothes, as well as safety glasses and protective gloves (rubber, latex or vinyl), because contact with the skin can cause long-term skin conditions. A suitable respirator should be worn to filter harmful fumes and, where possible, a fume cupboard should be used. If this is not available, work outside wearing a suitable respirator mask. Surfaces must be protected from spills by using a plastic tray; use glass or plastic containers to mix and store solutions. Spills should be cleaned up with newspaper and neutralised with bicarbonate of soda, it is a good idea to keep a supply of this to hand.

Always add acid to water, and add it slowly. Never add water to acid, this can cause a dangerous reaction. Whenever possible, choose a safer alternative if one is available, such as ferric nitrate crystals for etching silver, rather than nitric acid. Do not dispose of chemicals by pouring them down the drain; always dispose of them responsibly using an appropriate hazardous waste disposal method.

There are a number of less toxic, ecofriendly alternatives to chemicals. The most commonly used chemical in a jeweller's studio is pickle and there are a number of traditional, non-toxic pickles such as alum, citric acid and a vinegar and salt solution.

HEATING AND SOLDERING

Always set up an area on the bench using heatproof mats and blocks, several layers may be required to protect the bench top. A soldering table will raise the heating area. Extra care should be taken when casting; wear a leather apron and gloves for protection against the heat and splashes of molten metal. Gas bottles should be checked regularly for leaks by painting on a water and liquid soap mix, any bubbles that appear and grow are an indication that there is a leak and all connecting parts should be re-tightened and the safety check repeated.

CHARTS

RING SIZES

USA/ Canada	UK/Ireland/ Australia/ New Zealand	Europe	India/ China/Japan	Inside Diameter (in)	Inside Diameter (mm)	Inside Circumference (in)	Inside Circumference (mm)
½	A	38		15/32	12.04	1 31/64	38
¾	A½						
1	B	39	1	31/64	12.45	1 17/32	39
1¼	B½						
1½	C	40.5		½	12.85	1 37/64	40.4
1¾	C½						
2	D	42.5	2	33/64	13.06	1 41/64	41.7
2¼	D½						
2½	E	43	3	17/32	13.67	1 11/16	43.0
2¾	E½						
3	F	44	4	35/64	14.07	1 47/64	44.2
3¼	F½		5				
3½	G	45		9/16	14.48	1 25/32	45.5
3¾	G½		6				
4	H	46.5	7	37/64	14.88	1 27/32	46.8
4¼	H½						
4½	I	48	8	19/32	15.29	1 57/64	48.0
4¾	J	49					
5	J½		9	5/8	15.70	1 15/16	49.0
5¼	K	50					
5½	K½		10	41/64	16.10	1 63/64	
5¾	L	51.5					
6	L½		11	21/32	16.51	2 3/64	51.5
6¼	M	53	12				
6½	M½		13	43/64	16.92	2 3/32	52.8
6¾	N	54					
7	N½		14	11/16	17.35	2 9/64	54.0
7¼	O	55					
7½	O½		15	45/64	17.75	2 13/64	55.3
7¾	P	56.5					
8	P½		16	23/32	18.19	2 ¼	56.6
8¼	Q	58					
8½	Q½		17	47/64	18.53	2 19/64	57.8
8¾	R	59					
9	R½		18	¾	18.89	2 11/32	59.1
9¼	S	60					
9½	S½		19	49/64	19.41	2 13/32	60.6
9¾	T	61					
10	T½		20	25/32	19.84	2 29/64	62.2
10¼	U	62.5	21				
10½	U½		22	51/64	20.20	2 ½	63.1
10¾	V	64					
11	V½		23	13/16	20.68	2 9/16	64.3
11¼	W	65					
11½	W½		24	53/64	21.08	2 39/64	65.7
11¾	X	66					
12	X½		25	27/32	21.49	2 21/32	67.9
12¼	Y	68					
12½	Z	69	26	55/64	21.89	2 45/64	68.5
12¾	Z½						

Ring size is not the same as finger size, a wider ring will need to be larger than the finger size. A set of ring measurers or sizers should be used that are similar in width to the ring being made. Always add the thickness of the metal being used to the length of the ring blank.

USEFUL FORMULAS:

Circumference = 3.142 x diameter

Area = 3.142 x (radius^2)

METAL THICKNES: IMPERIAL AND METRIC CONVERSIONS AND DRILL SIZES

B & S Gauge	Millimetres	Inches Thou.	Inches Fractions	Drill No.
0	8.5	0.325	$^{21}/_{64}$	
1	7.3	0.289	$^{9}/_{32}$	
2	6.5	0.257	$^{1}/_{4}$	
3	5.8	0.229	$^{7}/_{32}$	1
4	5.2	0.204	$^{13}/_{64}$	6
5	4.6	0.182	$^{3}/_{16}$	15
6	4.1	0.162	$^{5}/_{32}$	20
7	3.6	0.144	$^{9}/_{64}$	27
8	3.2	0.128	$^{1}/_{8}$	30
9	2.9	0.114		33
10	2.6	0.102		38
11	2.3	0.091	$^{3}/_{32}$	43
12	2.1	0.081	$^{5}/_{64}$	46
13	1.8	0.072		50
14	1.6	0.064	$^{1}/_{16}$	51
15	1.45	0.057		52
16	1.30	0.051		54
17	1.14	0.045	$^{3}/_{64}$	55
18	1.0	0.040		56
19	0.9	0.036		60
20	0.8	0.032	$^{1}/_{32}$	65
21	0.7	0.028		67
22	0.6	0.025		70
23	0.55	0.022		71
24	0.50	0.020		74
25	0.45	0.018		75
26	0.40	0.016	$^{1}/_{64}$	77
27	0.35	0.014		78
28	0.30	0.012		79
29	0.27	0.011		80
30	0.25	0.010		

SILVER SOLDER MELT AND FLOW TEMPERATURES

Solder Type	Melt Temp °F	Flow Temp °F	Melt Temp °C	Flow Temp °C
Hard	1,365	1,450	741	788
Medium	1,275	1,360	691	738
Easy	1,240	1,325	671	718
Extra Easy	1,145	1,207	618	653

There may be some small variations in these temperatures depending on where the solder is purchased.

SILVER PROPERTIES

Silver Type	Alloy Composition	Melting Temp °F	Melting Temp °C	Specific Gravity
999.9 Fine Silver	99.9% silver	1,761	960.5	10.5
958 Britannia Silver	95.8% silver 4.2% copper	1,652–1,724	900–940	10.4
925 Sterling Silver	92.5% silver 7.5% copper	1,481–1,640	805–893	10.4
935 Argentium Sterling Silver	92.5% silver alloyed with copper and germanium	1,610	877	10.3

GOLD PROPERTIES

Metal Type	Alloy Composition	Melting Temp °F	Melting Temp °C	Specific Gravity
24-carat Gold yellow	99.9% gold	1,945	1,063	19.32
22-carat Gold yellow	92% gold alloyed with silver and copper	1,769–1,796	965–980	17.8
18-carat Gold yellow, red, white, green	76% gold alloyed in varying proportions depending on colour with silver, copper, palladium	1,598–2,399	870–1,315	15.2–16.2
14-carat Gold yellow, white	58.5% gold alloyed in varying proportions depending on colour with siver, palladium, copper, zinc	1,526–1,805	830–985	12.9–14.5
9-carat Gold yellow, red, white	37.5% alloyed with silver, copper, zinc	1,616–1,760	880–960	11.1–11.9

HALLMARKING

A hallmark is an official mark or series of marks struck on precious metal items to guarantee a certain pureness or fineness of the metal. The pureness or fineness is determined by formal analytical metal testing called assaying. Hallmarking regulations vary depending upon the requirements of the laws of either the country of manufacture or the country of import. It is advisable to check hallmarking regulations before offering items for sale as silver.

Hallmarking standards and regulations vary from country to country, for example in the UK under the hallmarking act of 1923 it is illegal to offer items for sale described as silver unless they have been tested and hallmarked by a UK Assay Office, exemption exists for silver items weighing less than 7.78gms. In the Republic of Ireland there is no weight exemption and all silver items intended for sale there must be hallmarked.

In 1973 a group of European nations signed the Vienna Convention on the control of the fineness and hallmarking of precious metals. This was intended to standardise legislation on the inspection of precious metals and assist international trade. The result was the Common Control Mark (CCM), which is applied to items that are assayed and conform to the legislation. In addition to this, a number of European countries have their own hallmarking systems; standards and enforcement varies from country to country.

A hallmark ususally consists of a series of marks that tell a story. In the UK, a hallmark is made up of four components: the sponsor (or manufacturer/maker) mark; the standard mark, which denotes the silver content of the item; the Assay Office Mark; and the date letter, which shows the year in which the article was hallmarked. The marks are applied either by a traditional hand-marking method using punches or by laser machine.

There is no official hallmarking system in Australia or the USA. In Australia, hallmarking is entirely voluntary and self-regulated with the marks stuck by the individual jewellers, however should the quality be queried there are strict laws that can be brought to bear if the marking does not match the assay. The USA has a similar system where the jeweller marks their work themselves with their name and a quality mark.

INDEX

ACKNOWLEDGEMENTS:

I would like to thank the following people: Xavier Young for his brilliant photographs and unending patience throughout the project. The talented makers who kindly responded to requests for images of their work and for generously allowing these to be used. Cynthia Eid, Stepan Terteryan, Kate McKinnon, Regina Schwarzer, Patricia Tschetter, and Ute Decker who generously shared their knowledge and expertise as profile makers. Cynthia Eid and Dr. Dorothy Erickson for their help with information from the USA and Australia. Clare Felgate at Argentium Silver for information on Argentium. Jessica Rose/The London Jewellery School, Michael Milloy, and Katy Hackney for the loan of some key tools. Cookson Precious Metals UK for help with materials and supplying the stone images.

My very grateful thanks to those makers who worked on tutorials, generously sharing their valuable knowledge and expertise and without whom this book would not have been possible: Melissa Hunt for Etching, Daphne Krinos for Stone Setting, Michael Milloy for Stamping, Scoring, Casting, Reticulation, and Filigree, Steven North for Engraving, Jessica Rose for Metal Clay and Wire Wrapping, and Adaesi Ukairo for Raising.

Finally thank you to my family, Andrew, Sam, and Tom, for their invaluable support and patience without which this book would not have been possible.

For more information about my work and for links to silversmithing suppliers and associations visit: www.elizabethbone.co.uk

TUTORIAL CONTRIBUTORS:
Melissa Hunt
www.melissahuntjewellery.co.uk
Daphne Krinos
www.daphnekrinos.com
Michael Milloy
www.m-milloy.com
Steven North
Unit 9, 43 Kirby Street, London

EC1N 8TE, UK
Tel. + 44(0)797 1722 531
Jessica Rose
www.londonjewelleryschool.co.uk
Adaesi Ukairo
www.ukairo.com

CONTRIBUTORS:
Jane Adam
www.janeadam.com
Cindy Ashbridge
www.cindyashbridge.com
Anne Bader
www.auri-jewellery.com
Talya Baharal
www.talyabaharal.com
Sun-Woong Bang
www.sunwoongbangjewellery.com
Kelvin J. Birk
www.kelvinbirk.com
Adele Brereton
www.adelebrereton.com
Shimara Carlow
www.shimara.com.au
Catherine Clark
cath53703@yahoo.com
Nancy Megan Corwin
www.nancymegancorwin.com
Ronda Coryell
www.rondacoryell.com
Donna D'Aquino
www.donnadaquino.com
Ute Decker
www.utedecker.com
Jörg Eggiman
www.eggiman-goldschmied.ch
Cynthia Eid
www.cynthiaeid.com
Celie Fago
www.celiefago.com
Darren Harvey
www.darrenharvey.com.au
Trudee Hill
www.trudeehill.com
Catherine Hills
www.catherinehillsjewellery.com
Kate Hodgson
www.katehodgson.co.uk
Birgit Holdinghausen
holdinghausen@optusnet.com.au
Melanie Ihnen
www.studio2017.com.au

Hadar Jacobsen
www.artinsilver.com
Mayza João
www.mayzajoao.com
Yumiko Kakiuchi
www.yumikokakiuchi.com
Christy Klug
www.christyklug.com
Hannah Louise Lamb
www.hannahlouiselamb.co.uk
Linda Lewin
www.lindalewin.co.uk
Terri Logan
tlstudios@aol.com
Jane Macintosh
www.janemacintosh.com
Susan May
www.susanmay.org
Wendy McAllister
www.wendymcallister.com
Kate McKinnon
www.katemckinnon.com
Suzanne Otwell Negre
www.suzanne-otwell-negre.com
Julia Rai
www.juliarai.co.uk
Todd Reed
www.toddreed.com
Nora Rochel
www.nora-rochel.de
Verena Schreppel
www.verenaschreppel.com
Regine Schwarzer
www.regineschwarzer.com
Erik Stewart
www.erikstewartjewelry.com
Stepan Terteryan
www.stepanjewellery.com
Patricia Tschetter
tschetterstudio.com
Estelle Vernon
www.estellevernon.com
Georgia Wiseman
www.georgiawiseman.com

OTHER CONTRIBUTORS:
Argentium International Ltd
www.argentiumsilver.com
Cookson Precious Metals
www.cooksongold.com
Xavier Young
www.xavieryoung.co.uk